CRYSTAL CLEAR JAVA

1ST EDITION

MOHAMMED ASHEQUR RAHMAN

AuthorHouse™
1663 Liberty Drive
Bloomington, IN 47403
www.authorhouse.com
Phone: 1 (800) 839-8640

Published by AuthorHouse 01/10/2019

ISBN: 978-1-5462-7177-2 (sc)
ISBN: 978-1-5462-7178-9 (e)

Print information available on the last page.

Any people depicted in stock imagery provided by Getty Images are models,
and such images are being used for illustrative purposes only.
Certain stock imagery © Getty Images.

This book is printed on acid-free paper.

Because of the dynamic nature of the Internet, any web addresses or links contained in this book may have changed
since publication and may no longer be valid. The views expressed in this work are solely those of the author and do not
necessarily reflect the views of the publisher, and the publisher hereby disclaims any responsibility for them.

authorHOUSE®

Crystal
Clear
Java

1st EDITION
Mohammed Ashequr Rahman

To my autistic son Anan who will never be able to read this book but has always been my inspiration and to my wonderful daughter Adrika who will be thrilled to see this book.

Preface

This book is about clearly understanding the concepts of Java as a language and then applying these concepts to develop applications.

The first objective of this this book is to make the concepts of Java language easy to understand.

The second objective is to make it easy to write Java solutions to a programming problem. Debugging and correcting your code quickly is also very easy at that point.

The third objective is to enable you to apply these concepts in learning another challenging language.

Finally, by the time you finish reading this book and practice the exercises, you will become a master of Java and ready to take on the next Java assignment.

About the Author

Mohammed Ashequr Rahman is an adjunct professor at New York University's (NYU) for over 20 years. During the last 20 years he has taught various courses at NYU including Java, Advanced Java, Java Web Services, JavaScript and Visual Basic. He has published a book titled "JavaScript Concepts" that is being used as a text book for JavaScript classes.

He has recently started teaching at Hofstra University.

Mohammed has a MS in Computer Science from NYU and has been working in IT field for the last 30 years.

He also has an MBA with a Finance major from SUNY, Stony Brook.

Mohammed is certified Project Management Professional and Oracle certified Java programmer.

Introduction

This book is broken down into two fundamental sections. In the first section, we will learn the basics of Java language. In the second section, we will learn how to use Java in multithreaded network programming environment.

All the examples in the book can be downloaded from the following link:

https://drive.google.com/file/d/1hRPyid-QsXC2fuPSF3CaoeUK8PrJpStr/view?usp=sharing

Contents

Section A

Java Language

Chapter 1

What is Java?

Image your computer is a deaf person that understands sign language only. What makes it even more challenging is that there are only two signs it understands "on" and "off". You hired this poor deaf person to work for you. As a manager, if you don't know how to express your instructions in these two signs of "off" and "on", so you can't get anything done by this worker. However, if you learn a language that can easily transfer your words to "off" and "on" instructions then you can express your instructions in that language and an interpreter will translate them to the computer's sign language and you are all set. Java is such a language that you are about to learn.

Java is an English like language with only 50 or so words in its dictionary. Using these 50 words we can express any computational instructions like "multiply 5 by 10", use an interpreter to convert these instructions to zeros("off") and ones("on") and send them to the computer to execute the task.

Java has the C/C++ language's look and feel but is much easier to learn and has a more consistent syntax.

Why learn Java?

To express your computational instructions, you need to learn an English like programming language that can easily be transformed to computer's language. Java is a relatively easy programming language to learn. Using Java you can develop any type of application starting from a cute little application on your desktop to a multi-tier robust enterprise application running on the web. When it comes to programming, Java is your "Jack of all trades as well as Master of all". Not to mention, it is by far the most popular programming language.

What is a program?

A program is a set of written instructions for the computer using a language like Java. A program is typically several lines of code. It is also known as "source code".

What is a compiler?

A compiler converts a program to machine language – zeros and ones. The compiler takes all the instructions in the program and generates machine code. Most programming languages like C/C++/Pascal uses compiler.

What is an Interpreter?

Just like a complier, an interpreter also converts a program to machine language. So, what's the difference? An interpreter takes one line of source code from the program and converts it to machine code. It then moves to the next line of source code and does the same thing again. Some programming languages like JavaScript uses interpreter and others use compiler.

What is the difference between a complier and an Interpreter?

Image you are going to write a paper on "computer security" for French audience but you don't know French, but you have a written script of your paper in English. You want to convert your lecture in French. You will use a compiler like "Google Translator" for the job. The compiler will translate your whole script and produce a French translation of the whole script.

In construct, imagine you giving an unscripted live lecture on "computer security" but your audience is French. You will need an interpreter to translate your words line by line as you speak.

So, both compiler and interpreter do the same thing, they just do it differently.

How is Java different from other programming languages?

Java, in fact, is very different from any other programming language in many respects. I guess, the most obvious difference comes from the fact that Java is compiled and run very differently from any language we know.

But first, let's take a traditional programming language like C. Here is how a C program gets compiled:

Any C program does not get converted to zeros and ones in one step. It needs at least two steps:

Step 1: C program gets converted into an assembly program. The generated assembly program is also a bit like English but ever more cryptic than the C program and has even fewer words in the dictionary.

Step 2: The Assembler coverts the assembly program into machine codes of zeros and ones.

However, the fact that an assembly program is generated in step 1 is already a problem.

Assembly programs rely on the underlying hardware. Therefore, for the same C program the assembly code will be different for different hardware. Subsequently, the machine code generated in step 2 is also different for different hardware for the same C program. This implies that a C program complied on a Windows machine does not run on a MAC or Unix machine and vice versa.

Java refuses to accept this shortcoming. Therefore, a Java programs can't be compiled in this fashion simply because Java is supposed to be machine independent. Java is supposed to be "Compile once, run everywhere".

Instead, here is how Java programs get compiled:

As shown above, a Java program gets compiled into Byte codes as opposed to assembly program. Byte codes are not machine dependent – they are sort of generic codes.

There is one big problem though. Because Byte codes are not zeros and ones, they are not meant to run on any machine and they don't. Byte codes are half-baked food, not ready for a meal.

So, how do you run such Byte codes then? Well, for the Byte codes to run on your machine, you must have an interpreter that will convert these Byte codes to machine codes on the fly, at runtime and feed them automatically to the machine. In other words, for your Byte codes to run, first you need to run a program called Java Virtual Machine (JVM) on your machine that works an interpreter. The JVM will convert your Byte codes to machine codes and feed them to your machine at runtime. Here is how it works at runtime shown below:

If you are familiar with any interpreted language, like JavaScript, this concept is probably familiar to you. The Byte codes are interpreted by the JVM. This means that any computer with a JVM installed can run Java programs, regardless of the computer on which the byte code was originally compiled.

For example, a Java program developed on a Personal Computer (PC) with the Windows operating system should run equally well without modification on a Sun workstation with the

Solaris operating system, and vice versa.

This is powerful stuff. This certainly gives Java the power of "compile once run everywhere".

A programming language usually needs a complier or interpreter – these two are mutually exclusive. Here we have a programming language called "Java" that uses both. Therefore, Java is very different from traditional programming language.

The good news is that Oracle provides the Java compiler and Java Virtual Machine (interpreter) for all types of machines for free.

What is Java Platform?

You probably heard the word "Java Platform" when you tried to learn Java first. So, what exactly is "Java Platform"?

Think of Java Platform as a packaged deal. The Java platform package is made up of three things:

a). The Java Compiler - "javac" program- compiles Java codes into Byte codes.
b). The Java Virtual Machine (JVM) – "java" program – the interpreter that converts Bytes codes to machine codes and feed them to the machine for execution.
c). The Java application programming interfaces(API) - commonly known as "Java API" is a set of compiled complex Java code, written by Oracle Java developers that you can use in your Java programs. So, in one word, the API is free Java programs written by experts.

The program I will demonstrate a bit later uses a Java API (System.out.println()) to print a line of text to your screen. We will compile this code using Java Complier ("Javac") and run it using Java Virtual Machine("Java"). All 3 them together is our Java Platform package.

Java Platform package is also known as Java Development Kit (JDK) and it is part of Java Standard Edition (Java SE) download.

In other words, 1) Java Platform 2) JDK and 3) Java SE – all 3 of them basically means the same thing. Confusing? I agree.

Downloads

To start learning Java, you basically need to download two things:

1). Java Platform package or the JDK
Go to Oracle's web site and download the latest JDK from Java SE download. Please make sure you download the JDK and not the JRE. The JRE only has the interpreter portion but not the compiler, the JDK has both and you need both. Please don't download JDK for Java EE either, that's for advanced Java programming.

2). Eclipse
Then go to Eclipse.org and download the Eclipse IDE for Java Developers. There is also Eclipse IDE for Java EE – please don't download that. Eclipse IDE for Java EE is for Advanced Java Enterprise Development. We don't need to get involved with Enterprise Development at this early stage.

Now you are all set.

Datatypes in Java

Words in human language can be categorized at nouns, verbs and so on. Similarly, every programming language has a predefined set of datatypes. The analogy is not exact but close enough.

Datatypes allow a programming language to classify data so that the compiler or interpreter knows how the programmer intends to use the data. For example, Java has a datatype called "int" shortened for "integer". Without getting into specifics, I can tell you that an "int" can hold a very large positive or negative whole number but fractions or characters wouldn't fit in integer. Similarly, Java has a datatype called "double" and it can hold a very large positive or negative fractional number but no character.

Java has 8 different datatypes, but they can be grouped into three types:

a). Six numeric datatypes (to store values like 23, 89.34 etc.):

    1). byte

    2). short

    3). int

    4). long

    5). float

    6). double

b). One Alphanumeric datatype called "char" (to store values like 'a' or 'm' or '2' etc.)

c). One boolean datatype called "boolean" (to store logical flags like true or false)

Datatypes are also known as Primitive Datatypes or simply Primitives. Here are the Primitives in Java:

Primitive	Purpose	Size	Minimum	Maximum
byte	Whole Number	8-bit	-128	+127
short	Whole Number	16-bit	-2^{15}	$+2^{15} - 1$
int	Whole Number	32-bit	-2147483648	2147483647
long	Whole Number	64-bit	-9223372036854775808	9223372036854775807

Primitive	Purpose	Size	Minimum	Maximum
float	Fractional Number	32-bit	1.4E-45	3.4028235E38
double	Fractional Number	64-bit	4.9E-324	1.7976931348623157E308
char	Alphanumeric	16-bit	Unicode 0	Unicode $2^{16}-1$
boolean	Logical True/ False	1-bit	–	–

Variables in Java

A program is all about processing data. Variables are the storage cells of the data processed by a program. You need variables in a program to hold the data values. The data could be the input to the program, output of the program or something in between. Regardless, you will need variable in all cases.

Imagine you want to write a program to that will square the number 3. This would be a very simple program. We will need two variables. One to store the input number 3 and one to store the output value (9 in this case). Here is how you will go about it:

```
int input = 3;

int output = input*input;
```

Notice how the variable "input" is declared and initialized. The datatype goes first, then the variable name, then an equal sign, then the initialization value. Also, notice how the variable "output" is declared and initialized. The datatype goes first, then the variable name, then an equal sign and finally the initialization by multiplying "input" by itself. That's square, isn't it?

Writing your first Java program using Eclipse

To write a piece of code called "FirstProgram" using Eclipse, do the following:

1). In Eclipse, select File → New → Java Project, type project name as 'CCJChapter1' and click Finish. Now project 'CCJChapter1' should be on the left-hand side of your screen. Select the project and right click on it.

2). Select New → Class and type class name as "FirstProgram" and check off "public static void main(String[] args)" and click Finish. The FirstProgram will be created in "src" folder under "default package" and you will have the following class created:

```java
public class FirstProgram {
        public static void main(String[] args) {
                // TODO Auto-generated method stub
        }
}
```

Between the curly brackets of main and below "//TODO Auto-generated method stub", type the following:

```java
System.out.println("I wrote a very simple program in Java");
```

Please don't forget to put the semi-colon at the end. Otherwise, the code will not compile.

Your program will look like this:

```java
public class FirstProgram {
        public static void main(String[] args) {
                // TODO Auto-generated method stub
                System.out.println("I wrote a very simple program in Java");
        }
}
```

Press Control + S (or click on the disk symbol on the toolbar) to save the file. In eclipse saving a file also means compiling it. If it does not compile, it will save the file anyway and will show errors with red x marks on the left side of the lines.

From Run menu select Run As → Java Application

Down below, on the console window you should see the output:

I wrote a very simple program in Java

Congratulations!! You have successfully compiled and interpreted your very first program in Java.

Chapter 2

Mathematical operators

In Java, the basic mathematical operators are the same as the ones available in most programming languages: addition (+), subtraction (-), division (/), multiplication (*) and so on.

Only one thing to remember is integer division truncates the result, rather than rounds.

For example:

```
int p = 14;
int q = 3;
int r = p / q;      // r will be 4 NOT 5
System.out.println(r); //prints 4
```

Java also uses couple of shorthand notation to perform an operation and an assignment at the same time. This is denoted by an operator followed by an equal sign, which I must say, looks really odd.

For example, to add 4 to the variable p and assign the result back to p again, we usually write:

```
p = p + 4; // increment p by 4
```

but in Java, you can also write:

```
p += 4; // increment p by 4
```

Auto increment and decrement

Java, like C, is full of shortcuts. Shortcuts can make code much easier to type but harder to read.

Two of the nice shortcuts are the increment and decrement operators (often referred to as the auto-increment and auto-decrement operators). The increment operator is "++" and means "increase by one unit." The decrement operator is "--" and it means, "decrease by one unit".

For example,

```
int b = 7;

b++; // b is now 8

System.out.println(b);
```

You can get the same result by putting ++ before "b" as follows:

```
int c = 7;

++c; // c is now 8

System.out.println(c);
```

Putting ++ before or after a variable has a slightly different implication in certain scenario but we will not get into that at this point to avoid confusion.

Relational operators

Relational operators generate a boolean result (true/false). They evaluate the relationship between the values of the operands. A relational expression produces true if the relationship is true, and false if the relationship is untrue.

The relational operators are less than (<), greater than (>), less than or equal to (<=), greater than or equal to (>=), equivalent (==), not equivalent (!=). Here is an example:

```
int b = 7;

int c = 7;

boolean same=(b==c); //using == to compare equality
System.out.println(same); //prints true
```

```
boolean different=(b != c); //using != to compare not equals

System.out.println(different); //prints false
```

Logical operators

The logical operators:

    a). && stands for AND
    b). || stands for OR
    c). ! stands for NOT

Her is an example:

```
int a = 4;

int b = 7;

int c = 7;

int d = 4;

boolean bothMatch=(a==d) && (b==c); //using && as AND
System.out.println(bothMatch); //prints true


boolean oneMatch=(a==d) || (a==b); // using || as OR
System.out.println(oneMatch); // prints true
```

int and double are Special Data Types in Java

You'll discover that if you perform any mathematical operations on whole numbers that are smaller than an int (that is byte or short), the resulting value will be of type int.

For Example:

```
short s1 = 1;
short s2 = 2;
short s3 = s1 + s2;      // does not compile
```

however,

```
short s1 = 1;
short s2 = 2;
int n = s1 + s2; // compiles fine and n is 3
System.out.println(n); //prints 3
```

You'll also discover that if you assign any fractional number to a variable, Java compiler automatically assumes that the number is a double and gives you error if the variable is not double. For Example:

```
double d = 9.1; //works fine
float p = 9.1;      // error because 9.1 is by default a double
```

A trailing "F" (upper or lowercase) fixes the problem.

For example:

```
float m = 9.1F; // works fine
```

Casting operators

The word cast is used in the sense of "casting into a mold." In Java, you can manually "cast" one datatype to another datatype (as long as it makes sense). You mostly do that to cast a higher datatype to a lower datatype.

Let's look at this example one more time:

```
short s1 = 1;
short s2 = 2;
short s3 = s1 + s2;      // does not compile
```

Obviously, the short variable s3 is fully capable of storing 3 but the compiler does not allow it. We can fix this problem by manually casting the result of the sum into a short as follows:

```
short s1 = 1;
short s2 = 2;
```

```
short s3 = (short) (s1 + s2); //casting int to short
System.out.println(s3); //prints 3
```

To perform a cast, put the desired data type inside parentheses to the left of the value.

We can also use casting to store a number in a float variable as follows:

```
float p = (float) 9.1;       // works fine because of the casting
```

if-else

The if-else statement is probably the most basic way to control program flow. The else is optional, so you can use if in three forms:

```
1). if(boolean-expression){
            statement1
    }
```

Or

```
2). if(boolean-expression){
            statement1
    }
    else{
            statement2
    }
```

Or even more complex,

```
3). if(boolean-expression){
            statement1
    }
    else if(boolean-expression){
            statement2
    }
    else if(boolean-expression){
```

```
            statement3
    }
    else if(boolean-expression){
            statement4
    }
    else{
            statement5
    }
```

Here is an example of main function that use "if" statement only,

```
public static void main(String[] args) {
    double d = Math.random(); // less than 1
    d = d * 100; // bump the number
    int i = (int) d; //casting to drop the fractional part
    if (i>50){
            System.out.println("large number : " + i);
    }
}
```

If you run the above code over and over, sometimes you will get an output like:

large number : 58

other times, the console will be silent if the random number is less than or equal to 50. We can fix the silence by adding an "else" statement as follows:

```
public static void main(String[] args) {
    double d = Math.random(); // less than 1
    d = d * 100; // bump the number up
    int i = (int) d; //casting to drop the fractional part
    if (i>50){
            System.out.println("large number : " + i);
    }
    else{
```

```
        System.out.println("small number : " + i);
    }
}
```

Now, you will, always get output indicating large or small number.

We can ever further fine tune the output by adding additional "if else" statements as follows:

```
public static void main(String[] args) {
        double d = Math.random(); // less than 1
        d = d * 100; // bump the number
        int i = (int) d; //casting to drop the fractional part
        if (i>80){
                System.out.println("very large number : " + i);
        }
        else if(i>50 && i<=80){
                System.out.println("large number : " + i);
        }
        else if (i>30 && i<=50){
                System.out.println("medium number : " + i);
        }
        else{
                System.out.println("small number : " + i);
        }
}
```

If you run the above code over and over you will get various outputs indicating very large, large, medium or small number.

Notice the curly bracket after every if or else statement. Although, sometimes you can do without them, please make a habit of always adding the curly bracket after every if and else clause otherwise you can easily introduce nasty bugs in your code that are very difficult to detect.

Debugging in Eclipse

Often, when you are constructing a logic you need to step through the code to see what is going on or why isn't it working. Eclipse does allow you to debug your code. Here is how it works:

Anywhere in your source code, you can put your cursor and hit Control + Shift + B or from Run Menu, you can select Toggle Breakpoint or you simply you can double click on the leftmost dark vertical bar right next to line numbering of your source code. Any of these would set up a breakpoint. A grey dot on the extreme left of the line will indicate that breakpoint has been set. You can setup as many breakpoints as you like.

Then, when you are ready to step through the code you can select Run→Debug As→ Java Application or simply click on the bug symbol on tool bar. Eclipse will probably ask you to change perspective, allow it to. Your code will stop on the first breakpoint. As this point, you can see the current values of your variables on the top right side. You can also put your cursor on a variable to see its value as popup.

```
1  public class IfDemo {
2      public static void main(String[] args) {
3          double d = Math.random(); //  less than 1
4          d = d * 100; // bump the number
5          int i = (int) d; //casting to drop the fractional part
6          if (i>50){
7              System.out.println("large number : " + i);
8          }
9      }
10 }
11 
```

You can select Run→Step Over or simply press F6 to move to the next line and repeat F6 on each line. If you found your problem and want to run the rest without stepping on each line, you can Run -> Resume or press F8 to keep running in normal run mode until the next breakpoint is hit. If you see a problem already and would like to stop execution, you can select Run→Terminate or Hit Control + F2 to stop execution.

If Eclipse does not automatically change your view back to original view, you can always select Window → Open Perspective→ Java to go back to the original view.

while loop

```
while(boolean-expression){
        statement
}
```

The boolean-expression is evaluated once at the beginning of the loop and again before each further iteration of the statement.

Let's look at the following example:

```
public static void main(String[] args) {
        double d = Math.random(); // less than 1
        d = d * 100; // bump the number up
        int i = (int) d; //casting to drop the fractional part
        while(i>1){
                System.out.println(i);
                i=i/2; //cut it in half
        }
        System.out.println("Exited the loop when i = " + i);
}
```

When you run the code, you will get outputs like:

```
71
35
17
8
4
2
Exited the loop when i = 1
```

While loops are great when you don't know how many times you have to iterate through the loop but you know the exit condition as is the case above.

for loop

```
for(initialization; boolean-expression; step){

    statement

}
```

A for loop performs initialization before the first iteration. Then it performs conditional testing and, at the end of each iteration, some form of "stepping". Stepping can be upwards or downwards.

Consider the following example:

```
public static void main(String[] args) {
        for(int n=1;n<11;n++){
                double m = Math.random(); // less than 1
                m = m * 100; // bump the number up so there is integer part
                int p = (int) m; //casting to drop the fractional part
                System.out.println(p);
        }
}
```

Every time you run the code, you will get exactly 10 random numbers, some of them could be duplicates but exactly 10 numbers.

For loop are wonderful when you know exactly how many times you want to iterate through the loop as is the case above.

With careful programming, everything that you can do with the for loop can also be accomplished using a while loop and vice versa. Therefore, they are interchangeable.

Infinite loops

There are times when you need to create a loop that never ends. Those are called "infinite loops". Here are the two infinite loop forms available:

```
while(true){
}
```

```
or
for(;;){
}
```

In the first case the condition to exit the loop is never false and in the second case the condition is missing altogether. Either way, these loops are infinite loop.

Breaking out of Infinite loops

Infinite loops are useless and will crash your JVM unless there is some exit condition inside the loop. How would you create such exit condition inside the loop? By using a "break" statement as follows:

```
public static void main(String[] args) {
        int p =0;
        for(;;){
                double m = Math.random(); // less than 1
                m = m * 100; // bump the number up
                p = (int) m; //casting to drop the fractional part
                if (p==50){
                        break;
                }
                System.out.println("p is not 50 yet: " + p);
        }
        System.out.println("Exited when p = " + p);
}
```

You will get an output that will look like this:

```
p is not 50 yet: 29
p is not 50 yet: 51
p is not 50 yet: 86
p is not 50 yet: 91
p is not 50 yet: 39
Exited when p = 50
```

You can do the same with an infinite while loop:

```
public static void main(String[] args) {
    int p =0;
    while(true){
        double m = Math.random(); // less than 1
        m = m * 100; // bump the number up
        p = (int) m; //casting to drop the fractional part
        if (p==50){
                break;
        }
        System.out.println("p is not 50 yet: " + p);
    }
    System.out.println("Exited when p = " + p);
}
```

switch

The switch can be sometimes be used as replacement for "if-else if" type of logic.

```
switch(a variable) {
    case value1 : statement1; break;
    case value2 : statement2; break;
    case value3 : statement3; break;
    case value4 : statement4; break;
    case value5 : statement5; break;
    default: statement6;
}
```

Let's look at the following example:

```
public static void main(String[] args) {
        double d = Math.random(); // less than 1
        d = d * 7; // bump the number up so there is integer part
        int i = (int) d; //casting to drop the fractional part
```

```
switch (i){
case 0:
        System.out.println("Sunday");
        break;
case 1:
        System.out.println("Monday");
        break;
case 2:
        System.out.println("Tuesday");
        break;
case 3:
        System.out.println("Wednesday");
        break;
case 4:
        System.out.println("Thursday");
        break;
case 5:
        System.out.println("Friday");
        break;
default:
        System.out.println("Saturday");
    }

}
```

The "default" clause is optional in switch, we could have easily said "case 6:" for Saturday and not have any default case at all.

You will notice in the above code that each case ends with a "break" (except for the last one). The "break" after each case is extremely important, if you forget, your code will continue to execute the next case (although the condition is not true) resulting in a very buggy code. This is called the "waterfall" behavior of switch and should be avoided by adding a break after each case.

Also notice, there is no way to use switch with > or < or !=, it only works with == conditions making its usage limited.

Commenting Your Code

Code comments are placed in source files to describe what is happening in the code to someone who might be reading the file. It can also be used to comment-out lines of code to isolate the source of a problem for debugging purposes.

The Java language supports two kinds of comments:

a). Double slashes

Double slashes (//) are used in the C++ and it tells the compiler to treat everything from the slashes to the end of the line as text. Here is an example:

```
//A Very Simple Example
```

b). C-Style

Instead of double slashes, you can use C-style comments (/* */) to enclose more lines of code to be treated as text. Here is an example:

```
/*
Here is where it all starts
A Very Simple Example
*/
```

There is a third type of commenting in Java for API documentation, but we will skip that for now.

Importing codes in your Eclipse

All the samples in this book are available for download as one zip file containing 12 zip files, each for one chapter. However, you don't want to unzip these chapter zip files. What you want to do instead is import them as Java Projects. Here is how:

a). In Eclipse, select File→Import

b). From General folder, select Existing Project into workspace, hit next.
c). Select the second radio button that reads "Select Archive File" and click Browse to navigate and find the zip file. Click on Finish.
d). Eclipse will import the whole project and it will show up on the left side of the screen.
e). Navigate to "src" folder of the project, click on "(default package)" and you will see all the .java files.

On the other hand, if you want to export your project from Eclipse as zip file to share with someone else or want to submit it for grading, here are the steps to get that accomplished:

1). Right click on the project, select Export.
2). From the General folder, select "Achieve File" and Click Next
3). On the next screen type in the location and zip file name and click Finish. You can also browse to find you folder and type in the filename after that.
4). Eclipse will create a zip file and export out of your entire project in it.

Chapter 3

What is a Function?

A function has a name and a purpose. For example, we can easily write a function in Java called "square". Obviously, the purpose of such function would be to square a number. If we send 3 to this function, it will compute 9 as the square of 3. If we input 7, it will compute 49 as the output. The computation inside the function could happen in one line of code or in many lines of code. Regardless, the function will work as a unit of code that we can execute by its name. The main purpose of function is to provide reusability of the code.

As it turns out in Java, all the codes we write must be embedded in functions. So, functions are essential in Java. Whenever we decide to do some computation in Java, we write the code inside a function and then we call the function by its name. In Java, you can easily recognize a function by its parenthesis right after the name of the function.

Here is an example of a function named "sayHello" that simply prints "Hello there!" on the console:

```java
void sayHello(){
        System.out.println("Hello there!");
}
```

Notice the parenthesis after the function name.

You have already seen a "main" function in the first example.

Some functions receive input – others don't. Some function returns data, others don't. Based on those two aspects, there are basically 4 different possible permutation of functions:

a). Our first function is a function that does not receive any external input and does not return any values to outside world, it simply executes some code. Such functions have the following structure:

```
void <function name>(){
// some code goes here
}
```

The word "void" indicates that the function does not return any value and the empty parenthesis indicates that the function does not take any input value.

Our "sayHello" function shown above is an example of such no-input, no-return function. The "sayHello" function has nothing in the parenthesis, indicating, it does not receive any input from outside. The function has the word "void" before its name indicating the function does not return anything.

This function can be then called from anywhere, if necessary, by its name as follows:

```
sayHello();
```

Notice the parenthesis is again needed to call a function, just the function name is not enough.

b). Our second function is a function that returns a value to the outside world but does not receive any external input.

Such functions have the following structure:

```
<data type returned> <function name>(){
// some code goes here
}
```

Here is an example of such function:

```
double getRandom() {
       double d = Math.random(); //calling another function
       double random = (d*100); // bump up the number
       return random;
```

}

The "getRandom" returns a "double" number indicated by the word "double" before the function name but does not receive any input from outside world indicated by the empty parenthesis. Inside the function, the statement "return random" ensures that the function returns a "double" number. Without that line the function will not even compile since it would violate the commitment to return a "double".

This function can be then called, if necessary as follows:

```
double myRandom = getRandom();
System.out.println(myRandom);
```

Notice the return value is saved in a variable myRandom. If we forget to save the return value, our code will compile and run but the returned value will be lost. So, it is important to capture the return value of a function if the function returns anything other than void.

    c). Our third function is a function that receives external input but does not return any value to the outside world

Such functions have the following structure:

```
void <function name>(<data type> <variable name>, <data type> <variable name>){
// some code goes here
}
```

Here is an example:

```
void changeStatus(int accountNumber, boolean isActive) {
//some code that change the status of the account.
}
```

Notice two comma-separated input to the function inside the parenthesis – an accountNumber and an isActive flag. Also notice the "void" return type indicated that the function does not return any value.

This function can be then called, if necessary, as follows:

```
changeStatus(1234,false);
```

    d). Finally, our forth function is a function that does both – 1) receives external input and 2) returns a value to the outside world.

Such functions have the following structure:

```
<data type returned> <function name>(<data type> <variable name>, <data type>
<variable name>){
}
```

Here is an example:

```
double getRandom(int lowerBound, int upperBound) {
        double d= Math.random();
        double random = (upperBound - lowerBound + 1) * d + lowerBound);
        return random;
}
```

This function can be then called, if necessary, as follows:

```
double myRandom = getRandom(30, 40);
System.out.println(myRandom);
```

We just learned all four flavors of functions and how to call them. We will learn more and more about these functions shortly.

What is User Defined Datatype?

We already know that Java has primitive data types like int, double etc. What is user defined datatypes then? User defined datatypes are available in other programming language but not in Java. However, discussion of user defined datatype is very important to understand some of the features of Java. So, we will discuss it here.

A user-defined datatype (also known as *record* or *structure* in other languages) is a way to bundle a number of primitive data types. This is rather hard to digest so we will start with an example.

Let's assume that we are trying to capture data about an employee. An employee has name, title, id, age, hourly rate etc. Let's focus on 3 easy elements: id, age and hourly salary.

We can capture his or her id in an int variable, age in another int variable and hourly salary in a double variable as follows:

```
int id=1234;
int age=27;
double salary=18.25;
```

We can also write a function to print all these data as follows:

```
void print(int anyId, int anyAge, double anySalary){
        System.out.println("Id: " + anyId);
        System.out.println("Age: " + anyAge);
        System.out.println("Salary: " + anySalary);
}
```

We can then call the print function as follows:

```
print(id, age, salary);
```

The function will print:

```
Id: 1234
Age: 27
Salary: 18.25
```

This is all good until a second employee shows up. Now we need another set of 3 variable to capture her data as follows:

```
int id2=6789;
int age2=24;
double salary2=19.50;
```

We can then call the print function as follows:

```
print(id2, age2,salary2);
```

The function will print:

```
Id: 6789
Age: 24
Salary: 19.50
```

So, for every employee we are creating has a set of 3 variables. Can we do better? The answer is yes. We can create 1 variable instead of 3. How? First, we need to create a user defined datatype called Employee as follows:

```
//this works in C++ but not in Java
Struct Employee
{
        int id;
        int age;
        double salary;
} ;
```

The code above basically says, "We are creating a user define datatype named Employee that is a bundle of 3 primitive variables: id as int, age as int and salary as double. These 3 variables that are part of a user defined datatype (id, age and salary) are known as "fields" of the user defined datatype.

Now we can do the following:

```
//this works in C++ but not in Java
Employee john;
john.id=1234;
john.age=27;
john.salary=18.25;
```

Notice the dot notion to access a field. We can now rewrite the print function so that it takes Employee as one argument as opposed to 3 separate arguments but still able to print everything we need as follows:

```
void print(Employee anyEmployee){

    System.out.println("Id: " + anyEmployee.id);
    System.out.println("Age: " + anyEmployee.age);
    System.out.println("Salary: " + anyEmployee.salary);
}
```

We can then print john's information as follows:

```
print(john);
```

When the second employee shows up, we do the following:

```
Employee barbara;
barbara.id =6789;
barbara.age=24;
barbara.salary=19.50;
```

We can then print barbara's information as follows:

```
print(barbara);
```

What is a Class?

User defined datatypes are powerful feature but powerful as they are, user-defined types present the programmer with one problem – the functions that work on these data types are separately kept from the data types – basically, the functions exist on separate files, separate folders etc. The connection between functions and user-defined types depends on the discipline, memory, and knowledge of the programmer maintaining the code.

Can we do better? Turns out we can. In Java, we combine user defined datatypes and the functions that operates on them into another bundle and we call that bundle a Class.

Please go back your project in Eclipse, right click on the project name and select new→Class. Type "Employee" as the class name.

Type the following code inside the class:

```
int id;
int age;
double salary;
```

Save it.

Your class will now look like this:

```
public class Employee {

    int id;
    int age;
    double salary;


}
```

The Employee class above is nothing but a user defined datatype at this point since it has no function. Now we will add the "print" function to it as follows:

```
void print(){
    System.out.println("Id: " + id);
    System.out.println("Age: " + age);
    System.out.println("Salary: " + salary);
}
```

So, your entire Employee class now will look like this:

```
public class Employee {
    int id=0;
    int age=0;
    double salary=0;

    void print(){
            System.out.println("Id: " + id);
            System.out.println("Age: " + age);
            System.out.println("Salary: " + salary);
        }
}
```

Notice, the print function is inside the class Employee. Also, notice the print function does not need any arguments, it can assess the fields of the class directly.

So, the difference between a Class and user defined datatype is that a Class also contains the functions (in Object Oriented Programming they are called methods) that work on the data.

Therefore,

Class = user defined datatype + function

Or

Class = fields + functions

Or

Class = fields + methods (another name for function)

Sometimes a Class may only contain fields and no function. Similarly, at other times a Class may only contain functions and no fiends. In other words, fields and functions inside a class are all optional.

Fields vs Local Variable

In Java, from location perspective, there are only two kinds of variables: 1) field 2) local variable. We now know what fields are. They are variables defined directly inside a class. So, what is a local variable?

A local variable in a variable defined inside a function/method of a class. Look the following example:

```
public class Employee {
    int id;
    int age;
    double salary;

    double calculateAnnualSalary(){
        double annual = salary*40*52; //40 hours a week, 52 weeks a year
        return annual;
```

```
    }
    void print(){
        System.out.println("Id: " + id);
        System.out.println("Age: " + age);
        System.out.println("Salary: " + salary);
    }


}
```

In this example, "id", "age" and "salary" are fields and "annual" is a local variable.

```
public class Employee {
    int id=0;
    int age=0;
    double salary=0;           Fields

    double calculateAnnualSalary(){
        double annual = salary*40*52; //40 hours a week, 52 weeks a year
        return annual;
    }                                Local Variable

    void print(){
        System.out.println("Id: " + id);
        System.out.println("Age: " + age);
        System.out.println("Salary: " + salary);
    }
}
```

In Java, fields are automatically initialized to their zero state but local variables need to be manually initialized. To avoid remembering this rule always initialize all your variables like we did above. All fields and local variables are initialized in Employee class – fields to zero value, local variable to a calculated value but initialized indeed. Now, you don't have to remember the rule.

Class Again!

Previously, we define class as user defined datatypes with functions in it. Although that is a correct definition of class, there is yet another way to define a class. This definition is dramatically different from the previous one.

A class describes a type of thing. Dog, in general, is a type of living creature. Therefore, Dog is a class. But my cute little dog "Max" is an object of that Dog Class. In other words, my Dog "Max" is an instance of Dog Class. Similarly, my Cat "Lilly" is an object of Cat class. From this perspective, a class is a "category". Dog, Cat etc. are just name of some categories, aren't they? The word "class" came from the word "classification" which simply means categorization. Therefore, when we organize things into different categories, the name of each category is a class and the things that we put in any specific category are the objects of that class. When someone casually says, "I come from a middle-class family", what is he/she saying? Well, he/she basically says that "middle-class" is the name of a class and that person is an object of that class. Does that make sense?

Here are some definitions of classes and objects:

- A Class is the cookie cutter and the cookies are the Objects out of that class.
- A Class is usually described as the template or blueprint from which similar Objects are made.

Class   Object

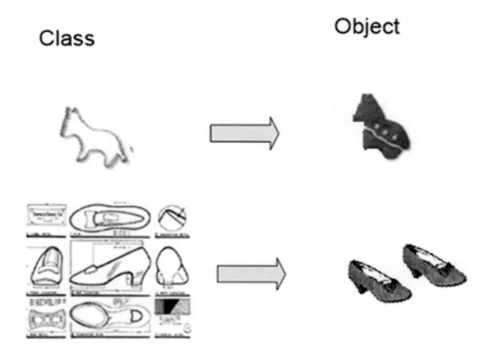

Creating Objects from Classes

In real life, the blueprint (class) of a building can probably be obtained for free but the actual building(object) will cost you millions of dollars. In Java, it is quite the opposite. Writing a class requires programming effort but creating objects from the class is piece of cake.

The creation of object out of a class follows this simple syntax:

```
<Class Name> <Variable/Field Name> = new <Class Name>();
```

Here is an example:

```
Employee john = new Employee();
Employee barbara = new Employee();
```

In the above example, the repetition of Employee on both sides of the equal sign seems to be redundant. This certainly needs some justification. Unfortunately, we have to wait for a while for the explanation.

Also, the parenthesis after Employee on the right-hand side looks very suspicious. Please keep an eye on this parenthesis because, in Java, parenthesis means function/method and we have not written any method named "Employee()".

Accessing Fields and Methods

In the above example we can create objects from Employee class and store them in variables like john and barbara. But how do we populate these objects with data like id, age and salary? How do we call a function like print() on these objects? The answer is: "using dot notation". Here are some examples:

```
Employee john = new Employee();
john.id=1234;
john.age=27;
john.salary=18.25;
john.print();
```

Similarly,

```
Employee barbara = new Employee();
barbara.id =6789;
barbara.age=24;
barbara.salary=19.50;
barbara.print();
```

Notice how we are accessing both fields and methods using dot notation. We can test that our code is working properly by following these steps:

In your project in Eclipse right click, select New→ Class. Name your class as EmployeeTester, check off "public static void main" checkbox and click finish. Inside the main function copy paste all the code from above so that your class looks like this:

```java
public class EmployeeTester {

        public static void main(String[] args) {
                Employee john = new Employee();

                john.id=1234;
                john.age=27;
                john.salary=18.25;
                john.print();

                Employee barbara = new Employee();
                barbara.id =6789;
                barbara.age=24;
                barbara.salary=19.50;
                barbara.print();
        }
}
```

Encapsulation

In the above example, we were able to create objects from Employee class and populate data on the object fields. The fact that we can access the fields of an object violates object-oriented programming principle. In object-oriented programming we are supposed to hide the fields of the object and provide functions (methods) to access them. This process of hiding fields and providing functions to access them is called encapsulation.

Private vs Public

To hide the fields of a class we have to define the fiends of a class as private. Private means "no access outside of the class". Consider the following BankAccount class:

```
public class BankAccount{
        private int accountNumber=0;
        private double balance=0;
}
```

The class has 2 fields and no methods at this point. Both fields are declared as private, therefore we can't access them anymore outside of the class. Our tester is now completely broken.

```
public class BankAccountTester {
        public static void main(String[] args) {
                BankAccount b = new BankAccount(); //complies fine
                b.accountNumber=1234; //does not compile
                b.balance=200.34; // does not compile
        }
}
```

The reason the code to access the fields of BankAccount from the tester does not compile is because these fields are private and not visible to the outside world. So, how would we assign account number to this bank account? How would we retrieve account number from this bank account object? The answer is by providing methods to access them. This type of access methods is called "getter" and "setter" methods. These accessor methods will be defined public. What does public mean? Public means publicly visible, anybody can access them. Here is an example:

```
public class BankAccount{
        private int accountNumber=0;
        private double balance=0;

        public void setAccountNumber(int anyAccountNumber) {
                accountNumber = anyAccountNumber;
        }

        public int getAccountNumber() {
                return accountNumber;
        }
```

```
}
```

Now we can modify the tester to use these methods to assign account number and retrieve account number as follows:

```
public class BankAccountTester {
      public static void main(String[] args) {
            BankAccount b = new BankAccount(); //complies fine
            b.setAccountNumber(1234); //compiles fine
            int myAccountNumber=b.getAccountNumber(); //compiles fine
            System.out.println("Account Number assigned: " + myAccountNumber);
//prints 1234
      }
}
```

What about the balance? How would we assign balance and retrieve balance? We can certainly create a similar setBalance() and getBalance() methods. While getBalance() method makes sense and we certainly will add such method but we rarely set balance of an account in reality. Instead, we deposit and withdraw from an account. So, a deposit() and withdrawal() method make more sense.

So, here is our new version of BankAccount:

```
public class BankAccount{

      private int accountNumber=0;
      private double balance=0;

      public void setAccountNumber(int anyAccountNumber) {
            accountNumber = anyAccountNumber;
      }
      public int getAccountNumber() {
            return accountNumber;
      }

      public void deposit(double anyAmount){
            balance = balance + anyAmount;
```

```
        }

        public void withdrawal(double anyAmount){
              balance = balance - anyAmount;
        }


        public double getBalance() {
              return balance;
        }
}
```

Here is our new Tester:

```
public class BankAccountTester {
      public static void main(String[] args) {
            BankAccount b = new BankAccount();        b.setAccountNumber(1234);
            int myAccountNumber=b.getAccountNumber();
            b.deposit(200.43);
            b.withdrawal(100);
            System.out.println("Account Number assigned: " + myAccountNumber);
//prints 1234
            System.out.println("Account Balance: " + b.getBalance()); //prints
100.43
      }
}
```

So, why is accessing fields directly prohibited? Well, let's consider the following business rule – account balance can never be negative. If we allow access to balance field from the tester, the tester can assign negative value to such field without a problem. However, by providing deposit and withdrawal function we can prevent balance from going negative by adding some additional checks in both deposit and withdrawal function. Also, our account number can also be negative since there is nothing stopping the tester from sending negative account number. We can stop that too. Here is the code that will stop account number and balance from being negative:

```
public class BankAccount{
```

```
        private int accountNumber=0;
        private double balance=0;

        public void setAccountNumber(int anyAccountNumber) {
                if (anyAccountNumber>0){
                        accountNumber = anyAccountNumber; //account number can only
be positive

                }
        }

        public int getAccountNumber() {
                return accountNumber;
        }

        public void deposit(double anyAmount){
                if (anyAmount>=0){//only positive deposit is allowed
                        balance = balance + anyAmount; // balance will always be
positive
                }
        }

        public void withdrawal(double anyAmount){
                if (anyAmount>=0 && anyAmount<=balance){ // can only withdraw if you
enough balance
                        balance = balance - anyAmount; // balance can be zero or
positive but never negative
                }
    }

    public double getBalance() {

                return balance;
        }
}
```

Now if we try to deposit a negative amount or try to withdraw a negative amount it will be stopped. Also, if we try to withdraw more than balance it will also be stopped.

Notice we have also protected account number from being negative.

Only private fields and accessor methods together can provide such protection, public fields can't. hence, it is the best practice in Java.

General rule of thumb, in a class, methods are public, and fiends are private. There are rare exceptions to this rule where some methods are private, and some fields are public but they are rare and we can discuss those exceptions later.

Constructor

In our BankAccount class, even after preventing negative account number, and negative balance, we still have some serious problems. For example:

a). Users can start depositing and withdrawing money using a BankAccount without ever assigning an account number.

b). The account number can be changed from one to another in the middle of deposits and withdrawals.

Here is an example where the user is withdrawing money but didn't supply any account number:

```
BankAccount b= new BankAccount(); //account number is zero

// money going into an account without any account number

b.deposit(100);
```

Or consider the following code where account number is changed right before withdrawal:

```
BankAccount b= new BankAccount();
b.setAccountNumber(1234); //good
bankAccount.deposit(100); //good
b.setAccountNumber(5678); //bad
b.withdrawal(50); // bad, money went out of a different account number
```

As far as Java is concerned, zero is a good account number. But that's not acceptable to us. We need a way to make sure that as soon as an object of BankAccount is created, the account number field is initialized to a positive account number. We can certainly introduce a check for valid account number in all appropriate methods, but Java offers a better and more centralized way to do the same – a constructor.

A constructor is a special method that is invoked automatically whenever an object is created from a class. Its job is to initialize the object (namely the fields of the object) to a valid starting state. The constructor must follow a standard name convention. Java could have called the constructor method as 'init' or 'start' but instead Java's designers decided to use the name of the class for the constructor name. Thus, a constructor for class BankAccount must be "BankAccount()" as follows:

```
public class BankAccount{
      public BankAccount() //constructor
      {
            //some code here
      }
}
```

Notice that constructor has no return type, not even void. A constructor can be declared as public or private; however, if we declare the constructor private, no one will be able to create an object of that class. Making a constructor private has some clever usage but that's rare and it is too soon to discuss such thing.

A constructor must follow the following two rules:

a). The name of the constructor is always same as the class name
b). There is no return type of a constructor – not even void.

Constructor with Parameters

Just like any methods, constructor may have zero, one or many input parameters. The constructor above has zero input parameter. For our BankAccount class, the constructor shown above will not be able to assign account number to the object since it does not know what the account number should be. It needs the account number as input parameter.

Here is such bank account constructor:

```
public BankAccount(int anyAccountNumber){//constructor with one input parameter
        if (anyAccountNumber>0){
                accountNumber = anyAccountNumber; //account number can only be
positive
        }
}
```

Notice the constructor code is identical to setAccountNumber() method (except it is missing void return type) and we don't need the setAccountNumber() method anymore. As a matter of fact, having setAccountNumber() method is dangerous now since it will still allow us to change the account number in the middle of transactions, so we will remove it. Here is the new BankAccount class:

```
public class BankAccount{
        private int accountNumber=0;
        private double balance=0;

        public BankAccount(int anyAccountNumber){ //constructor with one input
parameter
                if (anyAccountNumber>0){
                        accountNumber = anyAccountNumber; //account number can only
be positive
                }
        }
        public int getAccountNumber() {
                return accountNumber;
        }

        public void deposit(double anyAmount){
                if (anyAmount>=0){ //only positive deposit is allowed
                        balance = balance + anyAmount; // balance will always be
positive
                }
        }
        public void withdrawal(double anyAmount){
```

```
            if (anyAmount>=0 && anyAmount<=balance){ // can only withdraw if you
enough balance
                    balance = balance - anyAmount; // balance can be zero or
positive but never negative
            }
      }

      public double getBalance() {
            return balance;
      }
}
```

After introducing the constructor and removing setAccountNumber() method from BankAccount, the TestBankAccount tester is completely broken. The first line where it is broken is:

```
BankAccount b = new BankAccount(); //does not compile anymore
```

Why is this broken? If you carefully examine it, you will notice that we are calling the constructor after the word "new" but not passing any input parameter but account number input parameter is needed. So, we have fix it as follows:

```
BankAccount b = new BankAccount(1234); // compiles fine
```

We also must remove the code where we were calling the setAccountNumber() method:

```
b.setAccountNumber(1234); // remove this line now
```

After you take care of those two fixes your tester would work as before and look as follows:

```
public class BankAccountTester {
      public static void main(String[] args) {
            BankAccount b = new BankAccount(1234); //complies fine
            int myAccountNumber=b.getAccountNumber();
            b.deposit(200.43);
            b.withdrawal(100);
            System.out.println("Account Number assigned: " + myAccountNumber); //
```

```
prints 1234
                System.out.println("Account Balance: " + b.getBalance()); //prints
100.43
        }
}
```

Default Constructor

To create objects from a class, a constructor is a must. This statement seems hard to believe because, so far, we were able to create objects using our BankAccount class without defining any constructor. We didn't even know what constructors are.

Until now, the following statement worked just fine:

```
BankAccount b = new BankAccount();
```

It looks like we had a constructor in our class as follows:

```
public BankAccount() //constructor
{
        //some code here
}
```

Although we never wrote such constructor. In fact, we had a constructor. A BankAccount() constructor was *implicitly* declared for us by Java. This happens to every class. Until you introduce a constructor, a default no argument constructor is invisibly provided to the class. The best way to remember this rule is to remember the part of "Miranda warning" where the police says:

"You have the right to have an attorney. If you cannot afford one, one will be appointed to you". Same thing happens here:

"A Class has the right to have a constructor. If it does not define one, one no argument default contractor will be provided to the class by the JVM".

Here is the rule. If we do not explicitly define any constructor in our class, Java defines a no-argument constructor for us. It is also known as "Default Constructor" because we get it by default. The default constructor takes no arguments and does almost nothing (I said almost nothing since it actually puts one line of code but it is too early to discuss what that is). For now, the default constructor has no code in it.

However, the default constructor disappears from being generated by Java as soon as we declare our own constructor just like the court appointed lawyer disappears as soon as you hire your own lawyer. Capice?

Multiple Constructors

For certain types of bank accounts (for example CD) an initial deposit is essential to open an account. For other types of accounts (for example Checking account) the initial deposit is probably not mandatory.

To provide such flexibility, it sounds like we need a second constructor as well, one that takes account number and initial deposit as an argument. Java allows us to have multiple constructors for the same class.

Here is the second constructor:

```
//constructor with two input parameter
public BankAccount(int anyAccountNumber, double anyBalance){        if
(anyAccountNumber>0){

     accountNumber = anyAccountNumber; //account number can only be positive
  }
  // call the deposit function to put the money in
  deposit(anyBalance);
}
```

Now, we have two constructors for the same class, first one takes only account number and the second one takes both account number and initial deposit. Notice, we have two constructors that share the same name but different arguments. The question is, is it allowed in Java? The answer is, Yes. It is called "overloading".

Overloading

The fact that a single class can have more than one constructor as long as the constructors have different arguments is called "Constructor Overloading". However, overloading is not limited to constructors only. Methods can also be overloaded. Here is how method overloading works:

Within a class, two methods can have the same name as long as they can be distinguished on the basis of their distinct argument set. Let's see an example of method overloading.

In our BankAccount class, let's say we need to introduce interest rate with the following business rule:

If no interest rate is provided, a default current market interest rate (let's say 2%) will be assigned to the account and the setter method will return the interest rate assigned.

If an interest rate is provided, that interest rate will be assigned to the account.

At any time, the interest rate can be retrieved by calling an interest rate getter method.

Clearly, we can't accomplish 1) and 2) with one method because the arguments are different. These business rules can be easily achieved by introducing a private interest rate field, two public overloaded setInterestRate() methods and a public getInterestRate() method as follows:

```java
public class BankAccount{
        private int accountNumber=0;
        private double balance=0;
        private double interestRate=0;

        public BankAccount(int anyAccountNumber){ //constructor with one input
```

```
parameter
            if (anyAccountNumber>0){
                    accountNumber = anyAccountNumber; //account number can only
be positive
            }
        }
        public BankAccount(int anyAccountNumber, double anyBalance){ //constructor
with two input parameter
            if (anyAccountNumber>0){
                    accountNumber = anyAccountNumber; //account number can only
be positive
            }
            // call the deposit function to put the money in
            deposit(anyBalance);
        }

        public void setInterestRate(double anyInterestRate) {
            interestRate = anyInterestRate;
        }

        public double setInterestRate() {
            interestRate = 2;
            return interestRate;
    }

    public double getInterestRate() {
        return interestRate;
    }

    public int getAccountNumber() {
        return accountNumber;
    }

    public void deposit(double anyAmount){
        if (anyAmount>=0){ //only positive deposit is allowed
            balance = balance + anyAmount; // balance will always be positive
        }
    }
    public void withdrawal(double anyAmount){
        if (anyAmount>=0 && anyAmount<=balance){ // can only withdraw if you enough
```

```
balance
            balance = balance - anyAmount; // balance can be zero or positive but
never negative
        }
    }

    public double getBalance() {
        return balance;
    }

}
```

Here is the new tester:

```
public class BankAccountTester {
    public static void main(String[] args) {
        BankAccount b = new BankAccount(1234); //complies fine
            int myAccountNumber=b.getAccountNumber();
            b.deposit(200.43);
            b.withdrawal(100);
            b.setInterestRate();
            System.out.println("Account Number assigned: " + myAccountNumber); //
prints 1234
            System.out.println("Account Balance: " + b.getBalance()); //prints
100.43
            System.out.println("Interest Rate: " + b.getInterestRate()); //prints 2
            b.setInterestRate(3.4);
            System.out.println("Interest Rate: " + b.getInterestRate()); //prints
3.4
        }
}
```

this()

Since all the constructors initialize fields of an object, it is a very common that one constructor should call another to get most of the work done. After all reusable code is the best code.

A constructor can call another constructor by using the keyword this(). The keyword this() must appear as the first statement in the body of a constructor, otherwise the code will not compile.

In our BankAccount example, the second constructor is doing a little more work than the first one. We can easily modify the second constructor so that is calls the first one and then calls the deposit method as follows:

```java
public class BankAccount{
        private int accountNumber=0;
        private double balance=0;
        private double interestRate=0;

        public BankAccount(int anyAccountNumber){ //constructor with one input
parameter
                if (anyAccountNumber>0){
                        accountNumber = anyAccountNumber; //account number can only
be positive
                }
        }
        public BankAccount(int anyAccountNumber, double anyBalance){ //constructor
with two input parameter
        // call the first constructor
        this(anyAccountNumber);
        // call the deposit function to put the money in
        deposit(anyBalance);
    }

    public int getAccountNumber() {
        return accountNumber;
    }

    public void deposit(double anyAmount){
        if (anyAmount>=0){ //only positive deposit is allowed
            balance = balance + anyAmount; // balance will always be positive
        }
    }
    public void withdrawal(double anyAmount){
        if (anyAmount>=0 && anyAmount<=balance){ // can only withdraw if you enough
balance
```

```
            balance = balance - anyAmount; // balance can be zero or positive but
never negative
        }
    }

    public double getBalance() {
        return balance;
    }
    public void setInterestRate(double anyInterestRate) {
        interestRate = anyInterestRate;
    }

    public double setInterestRate() {
        interestRate = 2;
        return interestRate;
    }
    public double getInterestRate() {
        return interestRate;
    }
}
```

this

The keyword "this" (without the parenthesis) is used with fields and methods to refer to the current object. Here is an example:

```
public BankAccount(int anyAccountNumber)
{

        this.accountNumber=anyAccountNumber;

}
```

However, we don't have to use keywork "this" in the above example because Java implicitly uses "this." before the accountNumber and balance. Use of the keyword "this" in a method is helpful when a field is using the same name as a localt variable/argument within the method body. Here is an example:

```
public class MyClass{
        private long age=0;
```

```
public void setAge(long age){
        this.age = age;
    }
}
```

In the above example, with the statement this.age = age, "this.age" refers to field "private long age" but plain "age" refers to the "long age" argument of the method. However, using the same variable name for two different variables is confusing and somewhat bad practice. Please stay away from doing so and you will save yourself a lot of headache down the line.

Chapter 4

Memory Allocation in Java

Static and Dynamic Memory

Before we continue with our BankAccount class, let's take a moment and discuss memory space in Java. In any programming language like Java, memory is fundamentally divided into two sections:

Static Memory: In Java, whenever a class is referenced for the first time in a program, the class is loaded into static memory.

Dynamic Memory: Dynamic memory is divided into two sections:

Stack: Whenever a method is executed, memory must be set aside for its parameters and local variables. The area of memory into which a function stores its parameters and local variables is called stack. When one method calls another method, the second method's memory space stacks on top the first methods memory. If the second method calls a third one then the third on stacks on top the second one and so on. Hence, the name "stack".

Heap: Objects have fields – they need memory space too. The region of memory above the stack and in which objects can be stored is called the heap.

Static Field

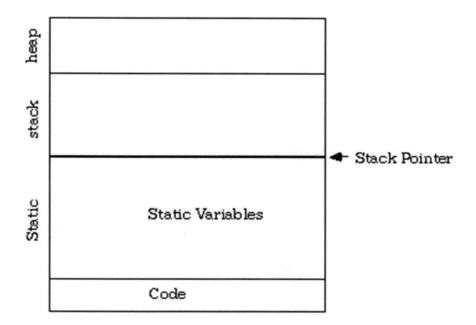

In our BankAccount class, even with the introduction of constructor, the way we assigned account numbers to the objects is not really very reliable. We might end up assigning the same account number to two objects because it is a manual process. It would be nice if the class could automatically assign account numbers in a sequential fashion. This task is very challenging at this point because we need a field that can be shared between all the objects created from the BankAccount class and every new object would increment that field value by one. So far, the fields we have seen belongs to one and only one object and the notion of shared field did not come to our mind.

This problem can be easily solved by declaring a private static field for the next account number in our BankAccount class. Static fields do not belong to any object, but they belong to the class. In other words, for all the objects created from a class there is only one copy of a static field and this static field resides in the class itself, which in turn, resides in static memory. That's why static fields are also called 'class level fields' while non-static fields are called 'object level fields'. OK, fine, but why private? Why not public? Because this is the most sensitive field of the class that keeps track of the next account number. We don't want anybody to tamper with this this field. We need to hide this field inside the class. Encapsulation all over again!

In our BankAccount class, let's introduce a private static field called nextAccountNumber as follows:

```
private static int nextAccountNumber = 1;
```

Watch carefully please. It looks like nextaccountNumber will be initialized to 1 every time we create an object from this class. But, the fact is, static fields are created and initialized only once, when the class is loaded in memory, no matter how many objects we create from the class, it will only be initialized once and once only. Perfect!

nextAccountNumber will be used and incremented by all the constructors of the objects we create from BankAccount class. Therefore, both the constructors should drop the account number argument because we won't use it any more. Instead, they will read the nextAccountNumber and increment by 1 for the next object.

Here is the change:

```
public class BankAccount{
       private static int nextAccountNumber=1; // class level fields to autogenerate
account numbers
       private int accountNumber=0;
       private double balance=0;
       private double interestRate=0;

       public BankAccount(){ //constructor with NO input parameter
              accountNumber=nextAccountNumber++; // assign account number
sequencially
       }
```

```java
    public BankAccount(double anyBalance){//constructor with one input parameter
        // call the first constructor
        this();
        // call the deposit function to put the money in
        deposit(anyBalance);
    }


    public int getAccountNumber() {
        return accountNumber;
    }


    public void deposit(double anyAmount){
        if (anyAmount>=0){ //only positive deposit is allowed
            balance = balance + anyAmount; // balance will always be positive
        }
    }
    public void withdrawal(double anyAmount){
        if (anyAmount>=0 && anyAmount<=balance){ // can only withdraw if you
enough balance
            balance = balance - anyAmount; // balance can be zero or
positive but never negative
        }
    }


    public double getBalance() {
        return balance;
    }


    public void setInterestRate(double anyInterestRate) {
        interestRate = anyInterestRate;
    }


    public double setInterestRate() {
        interestRate = 2;
        return interestRate;
    }
    public double getInterestRate() {
        return interestRate;
    }
}
```

The tester must be changed too, here is the new tester:

```
public class BankAccountTester {
        public static void main(String[] args) {
                BankAccount b = new BankAccount();
                int myAccountNumber=b.getAccountNumber();
                b.deposit(200.43);
                b.withdrawal(100);
                b.setInterestRate();
                System.out.println("Account Number assigned: " + myAccountNumber);
//prints 1
                System.out.println("Account Balance: " + b.getBalance()); //prints
100.43
                System.out.println("Interest Rate: " + b.getInterestRate()); //prints 2
                b.setInterestRate(3.4);
                System.out.println("Interest Rate: " + b.getInterestRate()); //prints
3.4

                BankAccount c = new BankAccount(300.89);
                System.out.println("Account Number assigned: " + c.getAccountNumber());
//prints 2
                System.out.println("Account Balance: " + c.getBalance()); //prints
300.89

        }
}
```

Static Method

Like static fields, methods can also be static. Just like static fields, static methods belong to the class rather than objects created from the class. Because of its location, static methods can only access static fields and other static methods. Static methods can never directly refer to object fields or object methods, even though these non-static fields and methods are located right next to the static method in the source code.

In our BankAccount class it would be nice if we could show how many accounts have been opened so far. Since the field nextAccountNumber is private – this information is not available to the outside world. We need a public getter method that will return this information.

Since the field nextAccountNumber itself is a static field, it is essential that we declare such a method as static.

Here is our BankAccount with static method:

```java
public class BankAccount{
    private static int nextAccountNumber=1; // class level fields to autogenerate
account numbers
    private int accountNumber=0;
    private double balance=0;
    private double interestRate=0;

    public static int getObjectCount(){
        return nextAccountNumber-1; //nextAccountNumber is 1 bigger
    }

    public BankAccount(){  //constructor with NO input parameter

            accountNumber=nextAccountNumber++; // assign account number
sequencially
        }
    public BankAccount(double anyBalance){//constructor with one input parameter
            // call the first constructor
            this();
            // call the deposit function to put the money in
            deposit(anyBalance);
    }

    public int getAccountNumber() {
            return accountNumber;
    }

    public void deposit(double anyAmount){
            if (anyAmount>=0){ //only positive deposit is allowed
                balance = balance + anyAmount; // balance will always be positive
```

```
                    }
            }
        public void withdrawal(double anyAmount){
                if (anyAmount>=0 && anyAmount<=balance){ // can only withdraw if you
enough balance
                        balance = balance - anyAmount; // balance can be zero or
positive but never negative
                }
        }


        public double getBalance() {
                return balance;
        }


        public void setInterestRate(double anyInterestRate) {
                interestRate = anyInterestRate;
        }


        public double setInterestRate() {
                interestRate = 2;
                return interestRate;
        }
        public double getInterestRate() {
                return interestRate;
        }
}
```

Since static methods are located on the class (not on objects), it makes sense that we should access such method using class name, followed by dot, followed by the method name. Here is the new tester that does exactly that:

```
public class BankAccountTester {
        public static void main(String[] args) {

                BankAccount b = new BankAccount();
                int myAccountNumber=b.getAccountNumber();
                b.deposit(200.43);
                b.withdrawal(100);
                b.setInterestRate();
                System.out.println("Account Number assigned: " + myAccountNumber);
//prints 1
```

```
          System.out.println("Account Balance: " + b.getBalance()); //prints
100.43
          System.out.println("Interest Rate: " + b.getInterestRate()); //prints 2
          b.setInterestRate(3.4);
          System.out.println("Interest Rate: " + b.getInterestRate()); //prints
3.4
          System.out.println("Object count: " + BankAccount.getObjectCount());
//prints 1
          BankAccount c = new BankAccount(300.89);
          System.out.println("Account Number assigned: " + c.getAccountNumber());
//prints 2
          System.out.println("Account Balance: " + c.getBalance()); //prints
300.89
          System.out.println("Object count: " + BankAccount.getObjectCount()); //
prints 2
    }
}
```

Static fields can be accessed using object variable names as well but it is recommended that class name be used as above.

Static Constructor

Simple static fields can be initialized during declaration as we did above. However, if the static field were an array, we would probably need a loop to initialize these fields. Similarly, if the static field needs to initialized using some kind of conditional logic we will need an if-else logic.

However, Java does not allow such a loop or if-else block of code outside of a method. To address this type of initialization problems with static fields, Java defines a static constructor for static members as follows:

```
static
{
      // some initialization code
}
```

The difference between a regular constructor and a static constructor is that a static constructor is executed when the class is loaded in memory, but a regular object constructor is executed when an object is created. That's a big difference! So, static constructor is only execute once in a application when the class is loaded but a regular constructor is executed each time an object is created.

For our BankAccount class we don't really need a static constructor, but we will introduce one anyway. We will initialize the static field nextAccountNumber to zero first and then in the static constructor we will set it 1. Here is the change in BankAccount:

```
private static int nextAccountNumber=0; // class level fields to auto-generate
account numbers
private int accountNumber=0;
private double balance=0;
private double interestRate=0;

static{
      nextAccountNumber=1;
}
```

Final Field

In Java, it is possible to declare a field as final. Final means that the value is not subject to change after initialization. Isn't that what constant means in other programming languages? Well, almost. Constants, in other programming languages, must be initialized as soon as they are declared. Final fields are a bit more flexible. A final field must be initialized either at declaration time or at the constructor. That's it, no later than constructor. The compiler throws error and refuses to compile your code if final field in not initialized past constructor. Here is an example of final field:

```
private final double defaultInterestRate=2;
```

Static & Final Field

Static fields can also be declared as final. This means three things:

1). There is only one copy of the variable per class, all objects from that class share that field since the field is static.
2). Nobody can change the value of the field once a value is assigned since the field is final.
3). Static final field is what constant is in other programming languages. It is to define a field whose value is set to stone once initialized.

The final field for default interest rate we declared above should really be static final since we only need one copy of it and should also be used in the setInterestRate() method to set the default rate. Here is our modified BankAccount class again:

```java
public class BankAccount{
        private static int nextAccountNumber=0; // class level fields to auto-
generate account numbers
        private int accountNumber=0;
        private double balance=0;
        private double interestRate=0;
        private static final double defaultInterestRate=2; // constant


        static{
                nextAccountNumber=1;
        }


        public static int getObjectCount(){
                return nextAccountNumber-1; //nextAccountNumber is 1 bigger
        }


        public BankAccount(){ //constructor with NO input parameter
                accountNumber=nextAccountNumber++; // assign account number
sequencially
        }
        public BankAccount(double anyBalance){//constructor with one input parameter
                // call the first constructor
                this();
                // call the deposit function to put the money in
```

```
                    deposit(anyBalance);
        }

        public int getAccountNumber() {
                return accountNumber;
        }

        public void deposit(double anyAmount){
                if (anyAmount>=0){ //only positive deposit is allowed
                    balance = balance + anyAmount; // balance will always be positive
                }
        }
        public void withdrawal(double anyAmount){
                if (anyAmount>=0 && anyAmount<=balance){ // can only withdraw if you
enough balance
                        balance = balance - anyAmount; // balance can be zero or
positive but never negative
                }
        }

        public double getBalance() {
                return balance;
        }

        public void setInterestRate(double anyInterestRate) {
                interestRate = anyInterestRate;
        }

        public double setInterestRate() {
                interestRate = defaultInterestRate;
                return interestRate;
        }
        public double getInterestRate() {
                return interestRate;
        }
}
```

String Class

Java has a primitive datatype char to hold only one character. Here is an example:

```
char c='h';
```

That's it. One character only! So, how do you store your name in Java? That's certainly more than one-character long. The answer is String class. You create an object from String class to hold unlimited amount of characters. How? You pass all your alpha-numeric characters to the string constructor within two double quotes as follows:

```
String myName = new String("John Smith");
```

This will create an object myName of string type and initialize with "John Smith".

Java also provides a shortcut for creating string objects as follows:

```
String myName = "John Smith";
```

Notice, there is no "new" just an equals sign will do the object creation.

String Concatenation

We know + sign add two numbers. It also concatenates two strings. In other words, the "+" sign is overloaded in Java. So is "+="; Here are couple of example:

```
String s1 = "hi" + " there";

System.out.println(s1); // prints "hi there"

String s2 = "hi";

s2 +=" there";

System.out.println(s2); // prints "hi there"
```

We will discuss String in detail later.

Arrays

An array is one variable that contains several slots to store several values. Simply put, an array is like a file cabinet with multiple drawers in it. When we create an array, we must specify how many slots we should have. Here is an example:

```
int[] myArray = new int[4]; //4 slots in the array
```

The [] syntax is to indicate an array, int[] means an array of int.

We will discuss array in detail later.

The "main()" Method

Finally, it is time to discuss the "main()" method. The tester classes have only one method "main" that has the following structure:

```
public static void main(String[] args){
}
```

The "main()" method is special. When run a tester, the JVM automatically runs the "main()" method. Why? We might think it runs the "main()" method because that is the only method in the tester class, but that's not the reason. Even if we add 20 more methods in our tester class, it will still run the "main()" method. Why?

A Java application is nothing but a collection of classes. Every Java application needs one class as the entry point. When we invoke the JVM, we pass the entry point class name to the JVM. For example "Java TestBankAccount". Here our entry point class name is obviously TestBankAccount. But just a class name is not enough. The entry class can have many methods in it, and JVM has no way of knowing which method to execute first. That is why, it is decided upfront by the Java designers that the "main()" method is the method that JVM will execute on the entry class. "main()" is the starter method of an Java application.

The "main()" method must be declared as follows:

```
public static void main(String[] args){
}
```

Let's do an autopsy of the "main()" method signature. It is a public method - that's why JVM could call it. It is static as well, which means it is a class level method, not an object level method. Because it is static, the JVM can call it without creating any object off of it. The return type is void, which indicates it does not return anything. It receives String[] – which in Java is an array of String (we will discuss more on String array soon). So, the "main()" method is a class level public method that returns nothing but receives an array of String objects and it is the entry point of an application.

Chapter 5

Pointer

Every field/variable/constant you declare is assigned a piece of memory. You can think of computer memory as a long city street (like Broadway in Manhattan). Each field/variable/constant in memory is like a house or store on that street. Each house or store on the street is assigned a unique address, like 240 Broadway. In case of memory addresses, it is a hexadecimal number like 0x1000. Let's look at the following code in main method:

```
int age = 30;
```

The statement can literally be broken down to two statements:

```
int age;      //Declaration

age=30;       // Assignment
```

The first statement reserves a piece of memory required to store an int (let's say 0x1000) and assigns it the name *age*. From now on, we can access the memory location 0x1000 using its name *age*.

The second statement says, "store a value of 30 at the memory location reserved by the name *age*."

Here is the picture:

Stack

Some languages such as C/C++ allow the programmer to access the memory location directly. Consider the following C/C++ code in main method:

```
int age = 30;

int* pAge= &age;
```

The first statement is the same as before, but the second statement says, "save the memory location of *age* (0x1000 is this case) in a variable *pAge*". Such variable is called Pointer. Here is the picture:

Stack

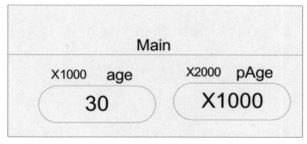

Notice how *pAge* has its own memory address as 0X2000 but it is storing 0X1000 inside it.

Now, let's look at the following C/C++ code in main method:

```
int age = 30;

int* pAge= &age;

*pAge= 67;
```

The first two statements are the same as before but the third one says, "assign the value 67 to the memory location contained in the pointer variable *pAge*" (0x1000 that is). This will change the value of age to 67.

Here is the picture:

C/C++ goes further than that and allows you move to the next or previous memory location by doing pointer arithmetic like pAge++ to go to 0x1001 or or --pAge to go to 0x999.

Fortunately, Java does not support pointers, therefore, there is no way to back and forth with memory address using pointers.

Reference

We just saw a mechanism of storing primitive data to a variable. *Object* variables, on the other hand, are created in a slightly different fashion. Consider the following example:

```
public static void main(String[] args){
        BankAccount citiAccount= new BankAccount();
}
```

Again, this statement can be broken down into two statements:

```
BankAccount citiAccount;
citiAccount = new BankAccount();
```

The first statement does two things:

1). It loads BankAccount class in static memory
2). It reserves a piece of memory (let's say 0x1000) in stack to store the memory address of any BankAccount object that is yet to be created. It assigns the name citiAccount to this address.

The second statement is little more involved. The right-hand side of the statement 'new BankAccount()' executes first. It goes ahead and takes the memory it needs from a special pool of memory that Java controls called the heap and creates a new object of BankAccount type. Once that's done, it returns the memory address of heap that is taken by the new object. At this point, the left-hand side of the statement is executed, it simply stores the heap address to the variable citiAccount. Here is the picture:

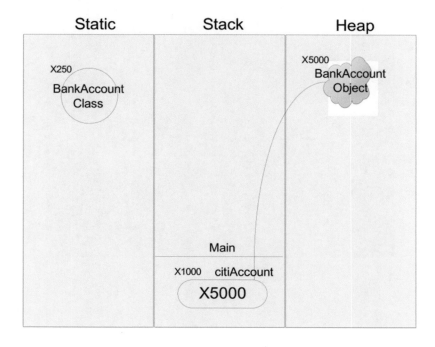

So, citiAccount is surely a pointer. It is a pointer to an object, BankAccount object. In other words, in Java, pointers can only be pointing to objects, and they are called References. In C/C++ pointer arithmetic like ++,-- etc. can move the pointed back and forth but in Java References can't be used for such operations.

You can think of Reference variables as names for an object. Let's say, I have a cat. The cat is an object. His name is "Jack". Jack is a reference to the cat object. I can give my cat many names and they all are going to point to the same object – my cat Jack. Consider the following example:

```
BankAccount citiAccount= new BankAccount();

BankAccount chaseAccount = citiAccount;
```

Now, chaseAccount and citiAccount are both referring to the same object in the heap. We just made two references to the same object. Here is the picture:

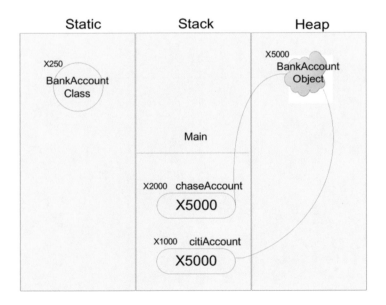

Arrays

An array object contains a collection of values. Think of an array as file cabinet with multiple drawers. The drawers have no names; instead they are referenced by numeric indexes. If an array has n drawers, we say the array has a length of n or size of n and each drawer have an index from 0 to n-1. All the drawers of an array can contain values of the same type.

Although arrays are objects they are declared and created with a slightly different syntax. The following declares a variable that will contain reference to an array of integers:

```
int myIntArray[];
```

The brackets indicate that this is a reference to an array. The brackets can be placed either before or after the reference name as follows:

```
Int[] myIntArray;
```

My recommendation is that you follow the second syntax like int[], the reason for that will become clear soon.

Before you can use this array variable for any practical purposes, you must create the array object with the "new" keyword but there is one more thing. In addition to the "new" keyword you also must declare the size of the array as follows:

```
myIntArray = new int[3];
```

You just created an array object of size 3. In other words, you just created a file cabinet with 3 drawers.

You can do the two steps in one as follows:

```
int[] myIntArray = new int[3];
```

Now that we have an array of integers, we can individually assign values to each element of the array as follows:

```
myIntArray[0]=5; // first drawer stores number 5

myIntArray[1]=10; //  second drawer stores number 10

myIntArray[2]=15; //  third drawer stores number 15

System.out.println(myIntArray[1]); //prints 10

System.out.println(myIntArray[2]); //prints 15

System.out.println(myIntArray[0]); //prints 5
```

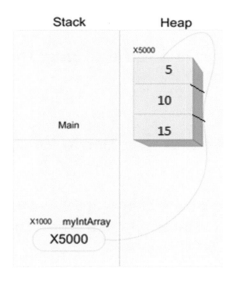

If you know the array element values beforehand, Java provides a shortcut for both creating the array and assigning values in one step:

```
int anotherIntArray[] = {7,3,18};
```

The statement above will create an array of size 3 and assign the values on the elements 0,1,2 in order. Arrays have a length field that keeps the count of elements in the array. Here is a check:

```
System.out.println(anotherIntArray[0]); //prints 7

System.out.println(anotherIntArray[1]); //prints 3

System.out.println(anotherIntArray[2]); //prints 18

System.out.println(anotherIntArray.length); //prints 3
```

In Java, arrays are fixed size - you cannot change the size of the array after creation, but you can change the values in each slot.

Arrays Containing Objects

Arrays containing objects are a bit tricky to understand. Let's look at the following example:

```
public static void main(String[] args){

        BankAccount bankAccountArray[] = new BankAccount[3];

}
```

Again, it can be broken down into two statements:

```
BankAccount[] bankAccountArray;

bankAccountArray = new BankAccount[3];
```

The first statement reserves a piece of memory (let's say 0x1000) required to store the memory address of an array object. Then it assigns a name bankAccountArray to it.

The second statement: The right-hand side of the statement 'new BankAccount[3]' executes first. It goes ahead and takes the memory it needs to hold a file cabinet in the heap. Once that's done, it returns the memory address of heap that is taken by the new object array. At this point, the left-hand side simply saves the heap address to the variable bankAccountArray.

Here is an interesting question. At this point, how many BankAccount object have we created? Three? One? None? The right answer is, NONE. We merely created a file cabinet that is capable of storing references to three BankAccount objects, but we haven't created a single BankAccount yet.

Consider the following statement now:

```
bankAccountArray[0] = new BankAccount(500);
```

The-right hand side of the statement 'new BankAccount(500)' executes first. It goes ahead and takes the memory it needs to hold a new BankAccount on the heap and creates a new object of BankAccount type. Once that's done, it returns the memory address of heap that is taken by the new BankAccount object. At this point, the left-hand side simply saves the heap address of the BankAccount object to slot 0 of bankAccountArray. Right now, bankAccountArray is holding a reference of a BankAccount at slot 0. The other two slots are still empty. Here is the picture:

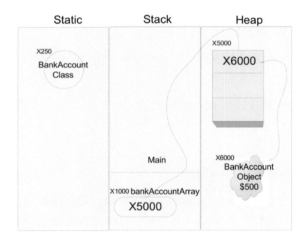

How many objects are on the heap now? Only two. One Array and one BankAccount.

Now, let's do the following:

```
bankAccountArray[2] = bankAccountArray[0];
```

What is bankAccountArray[0] again? It is a reference to a BankAccount object somewhere on the heap that has $500 initial deposit. What does bankAccountArray[2] get? It gets a copy of the reference to the same BankAccount object.

Once again, how many objects do we have in the heap now? The answer is two, still two, we have not created any new object in the last statement. Here is the picture:

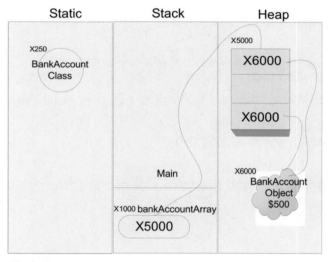

If we run the following statements ...

```
System.out.println("Account Number in bankAccountArray[2] is: " +
bankAccountArray[2].getAccountNumber()); //prints 1
```

```
System.out.println("Account Number in bankAccountArray[0] is: " +
bankAccountArray[0]. getAccountNumber()); // prints 1
```

We will get the exact same account number, since they are both pointing to the same exact object.

Now, if we run:

```
bankAccountArray[2].deposit(700);
```

```
System.out.println("Balance in bankAccountArray[2] is: "
```

```
+ bankAccountArray[2].getBalance()); //prints 1200
```

we get,

Balance in bankAccountArray[2] is: 1200.0

That makes sense, after all $500 + $700 is $1200.

Fine. If we run the following statement …

```
System.out.println("Balance in bankAccountArray[0] is: " +
bankAccountArray[0].getBalance()); //prints 1200          private long age=0;
```

Notice, we are using the zero slot this time. What should we get? We will get,

Balance in bankAccountArray[0] is: 1200.0

How come? Because the first slot and the third slot of the array are sharing the same object. Here is the updated picture:

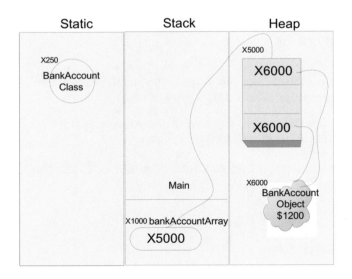

Imagine now, we run the following code:

```
bankAccountArray[2] = new BankAccount(800);

System.out.println("Account Number in bankAccountArray[2] is: " +
bankAccountArray[2].getAccountNumber()); // prints 2

System.out.println("Balance in bankAccountArray[2] is: " +
bankAccountArray[2].getBalance()); //prints 800
```

bankAccountArray[2] will suddenly refer to a new object with different account number and initial deposit of $800.

Here is the picture:

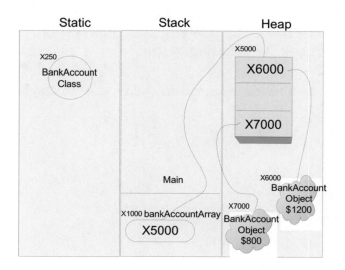

The Array Class

We know now that arrays are objects. If arrays are objects, where is the array class? Who created these array classes? Good question. Think of it this way: for every primitive data type like int, double etc. there is a corresponding built-in array class like int[],double[] etc.

For object types, every time we create a class, Java automatically creates a corresponding array class. When we create BankAccount class, immediately an array class named BankAccount[] is created. This is what I call "Buy a class, get an array for free". The underlying mechanism for array is a bit complicated than this but this understanding is good enough for all practical purposes.

One final observation. The statement:

```
int[] myIntArray = new int[10];
```

should really be read as:

```
int[] myIntArray = new int[](10); //does not compile
```

Here, the class name is int[] and we are creating a new object myIntArray from the class int[], which has a constructor (with parenthesis) that takes number of elements as an argument, and we are passing 10. Makes sense? Unfortunately, Java (just like C/C++) does not create array objects using this syntax. It uses the following syntax:

```
int[] myIntArray = new int[10];//no parenthesis for the constructor call, the input
parameter goes inside [] instead of ()
```

Chapter 6

Strings from an immutable prospective

We already discussed String briefly. Objects from String class enables us to store a string of alphanumeric characters like your name or VIN number of a car. However, in Java, strings are immutable. Which means strings are constant; once created, their values cannot be changed. Initially, that sounds ok until you find out that strings have methods like toUpperCase() or toLowercase(). If a string is so immutable, what do these methods do? Let's try this:

```
String nameString="john";
nameString.toUpperCase();
System.out.println(nameString);
```

What's the output? The output is still "john" (in lowercase). What happened to upper casing? What did we do wrong?

Let's try it again now, this time slightly differently:

```
String nameString="John";
String anotherNameString=nameString.toUpperCase();
System.out.println(anotherNameString);
```

What's the output? Sure, it is "JOHN" (in uppercase), as we would normally expect. How come? What happened to immutability now?

Before I explain what's happening here let's look at something else. When we call a method on an object the method operates on the object itself. For example:

```
citiAccount.deposit(500);
```

This will increment the balance field of citiAccount by 500. In other words, the deposit() method works on the citiAccount object itself. In other words, citiAccount is mutable.

However, in case of toUpperCase() of string that's not the case. The toUpperCase() method looks at every character in original string, coverts it to upper case and puts in another new string object located in a different memory location in heap and then returns the address of the new string object. It never touches the original string object.

In the first example we did not save the returned value of toUpperCase() method. Therefore, nameString is still pointing to "john" and the newly created "JOHN" is not at all referenced.

Here is the picture:

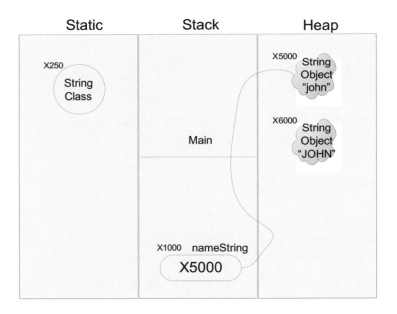

In the second example, we assigned the newly created string object to another variable anotherNameString – that's what made it look like we changed the original string "john" to "JOHN". In fact, if we run the following code:

```
System.out.println(nameString);
```

We will see that "john" is indeed unchanged. if we can search the heap, we will find that both "john" and "JOHN" exist as two separate objects.

Here is the picture:

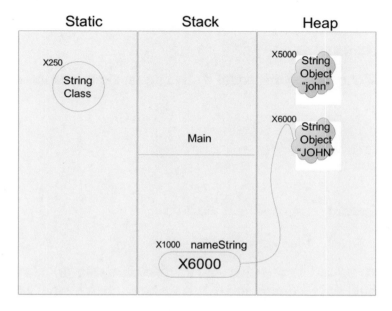

In other words, all the methods of String class operate on a copy of the original object, and never touch the original object, making strings immutable.

substrings() method of String

At first string's substring(int beginIndex, int endIndex) method looks fairly straightforward. If returns another string found between the beginIndex and endIndex location. Let's put it to test:

```java
String original ="ABCDEF";
String sub = original.substring(0,3);
System.out.println(sub);
```

Knowing that string's index is zero based we can quickly conclude that sub will contain "ABCD" – characters located at 0,1,2 and 3 locations – total of 4 characters. However, if we run the code we will see that it contains "ABC" – characters located at 0, 1 and 2 locations– total of 3 characters. Why? Well, string designers design the substring() method such that it never goes to endIndex, it stops at endIndex minus one location. Design flaw? We can certainly say so but that does not change the output. We have to live with this flaw of Java.

String and = = Operator

In Java you compare if two values are equal by two equal signs as follows:

```
int i = 9;
int j = 9;
if (i == j){
      System.out.println("They are equal");
}
else{
      System.out.println("They are not equal");
}
```

The output is "They are equal". In other words, it works fine with primitive data type. However, objects (like string) should not be compared in this fashion. Let's try this with two string variables instead:

```
String name1="john";

String name2="john";

if (name1 == name2){
      System.out.println("Equal");
}
else{
      System.out.println("Not Equal");
}
```

As we expected, the output is indeed "Equal", so the two equals sign does work for strings! Not so fast. Let's try the example in a slightly different fashion:

```
String name1=new String("john");
String name2=new String("john");
if (name1 == name2){
```

```java
        System.out.println("Equal");
}
else{
        System.out.println("Not Equal");
}
```

Surprisingly, this time the output is "Not Equal". How come? The answer is little complicated. In the first case there is only one string object "john" and both name1 and name2 are references to the same object. Here is the picture:

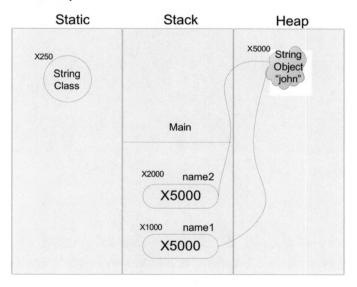

However, in the second case, both the first statement and the second statement create two separate new strings in two separate memory addresses. Therefore, the reference in variable name1 is different from the reference in variable name2. Here is the picture:

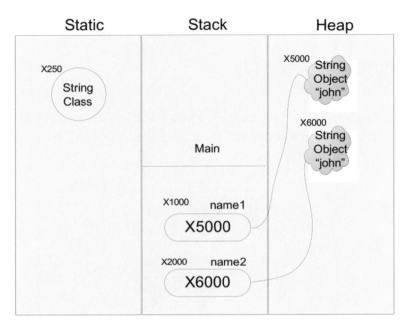

Furthermore, the statement:

```
if (name1 == name2){
```

Compares the two memory addresses. Since one is 0x5000 and the other is 0X6000, they don't match, and the result is "Not Equal". So, how would we ever compare two strings reliably? The answer is equals() method of string. String has a equals() method that can compare one string with another regardless of their memory location. Here is the correct code:

```
if (name1.equals(name2)){
        System.out.println("Equal");

}
else{
        System.out.println("Not Equal");

}
```

This will always return true as long as name1 and name2 contains the same set of characters in the same order.

Going back to the original example:

```
String name1="john";
String name2="john";
```

How does Java dare to reference the same object by two variables name1 and name2? Shouldn't they be two new string objects? Yes, but strings are immutable or constants, so Java figures there is no need to create two copies of the same constant "john", one is enough and let's just reuse it over and over.

Parameter Passing in Java

When we invoke a method and the method expects input parameters, we have to pass the parameters with the method call as follows:

```
String original ="ABCDEF";
String sub = original.substring(0,3);
```

Notice we are passing 0 and 3 to the method substring as parameters. Now, let's take this example:

```
public static void main(String[] args){
      int age=30;
      updateAge(age);
      System.out.println(age); // what is printed, 30 or 45?
}
public static void updateAge(int newAge){
      newAge = 45;
}
```

What should be printed on the monitor? The correct answer is it depends on how parameters are being passed.

1). If "age" is passed by value, then "newAge" will receive 30 from "age" and then it will change its value to 45. The value of "age" will still be untouched, and the output to the monitor will be 30.

2). However, if "age" is passed by reference, then "newAge" will receive the reference of "age" (let's say 0x1000) and newAge will write 45 to that memory address (0x1000), and at the end both age and newAge will be 45. The output to the monitor will be 45.

Now that we know what could possibly happen, the question is, what really happens in Java? The answer is 1) happens, age is passed by value. So, primitives are passed by value.

Let's look at another example:

```java
public static void main(String[] args){
    BankAccount b=new BankAccount();

    updateBalance(b);

    System.out.println(b.getBalance()); // what is printed, 0 or 500?
}
public static void updateBalance(BankAccount anyAccount){
    anyAccount.deposit(500);

}
```

What is printed? 0 or 500. The answer is of course 500. The reference to b (let's say 0x2000) is passed to anyAccount. Therefore, b and anyAccount are two references to the same object. So, objects are passed by reference.

There are two distinct camps on this matter. They both say the same thing, but they say it completely differently:

Group A:

1). Java passes primitive data type parameters (int, double etc) by value. So, in the above example 30 will be printed on the Monitor.

2). Java passes object data type parameters (String objects, BankAccount objects) by reference. Remember, object variable only has a reference to the object. It does not have the actual object – the actual object is in heap. Therefore, it must pass the reference to the object.

Group B:

Java passed everything by value.

1). When the parameter is of primitive data type, the receiving variable (argument) gets a local copy the value.
2). However, if the variables happen to be an object variable, its value is a memory address to an object (let's say 0x2000), and the receiving variable gets a local copy of the memory address (0x2000).

Both groups have valid points and it does not really matter which version of the interpretation you accept. The most important thing is to understand the fact that when an object variable is passed to a method as a parameter, the method can change the state of the object, unless the object is immutable.

StringBuilder

A StringBuilder is everything you expected string to be. A StringBuilder implements a mutable sequence of characters. A StringBuilder is like a string but can be modified. At any point in time, it contains a sequence of characters, but the length and content of the sequence can be changed through certain method calls.

The principal operations on a StringBuilder are the append and insert methods, which are overloaded to accept data of any type. The append() method always adds these characters at the end of the buffer; the insert() method adds the characters at a specified point.

Every StringBuilder has a capacity. If the internal buffer overflows, the capacity is automatically made larger.

Here is an Example of StringBuilder:

```
public static void main(String[] args) {
        StringBuilder sb = new StringBuilder("Hi"); // "Hi"
        System.out.println(sb);
        sb.append(",how are you?");    //"Hi, how are you?"
        System.out.println(sb);
        sb.insert(3,"John"); //"Hi John, how are you?"
        System.out.println(sb);
}
```

If you are working in a multi-threaded environment, you may want to use StringBuffer instead of StringBuilder. We will discuss multi-threaded programming later.

Wrapper Classes for Primitive Data Types

In a pure object-oriented programming language everything should be classes and objects – there should be no primitive datatypes. However, Java introduced primitives to avoid some slowness in execution. For that reason, Java is not pure object-oriented programming language but close enough. Java compensates for this short-coming by proving Wrapper Classes. There is a Wrapper Class for each primitive datatype. The main purpose of having these Wrapper Classes is to convert primitive data to objects, in other words, to wrap primitives by objects.

By the way, objects from these wrapper classes are immutable like string.

Each of these wrapper classes has two constructors:

a). Takes the primitive data as an argument, converts it to an object.
b). Takes a string as an argument, converts it to an object. If the string can't be converted to primitive data, it throws an error message at runtime.

Each of these wrapper classes has a xxxValue() method that converts it back to primitive data. "xxx" stands for primitive datatype.

Here is the complete list of these wrapper classes:

Primitive Data Type	Wrapper Class	Special Methods
boolean	Boolean	booleanValue() - Returns boolean
char	Character	charValue() - Returns char
byte	Byte	byteValue() - Returns byte
short	Short	shortValue() - Returns short
int	Integer	intValue() - Returns int
long	Long	longValue() - Returns long
float	Float	floatValue() - Returns float
double	Double	doubleValue() - Returns double

Here is an example:

```
public static void main(String[] args) {
      int intInput = 100;
      Integer intWrapped = null;
      int intOutput = 0;

      intWrapped = new Integer(intInput);
      intOutput = intWrapped.intValue();
      System.out.println(intOutput);

      double doubleInput = 200.34;
```

```
        Double doubleWrapped = null;
        double doubleOutput = 0;


        doubleWrapped = new Double(doubleInput);
        doubleOutput = doubleWrapped.doubleValue();
        System.out.println(doubleOutput);
}
```

Boxing

Since JDK 1.5 Java introduced boxing. Boxing, also known as Auto-boxing, allows smooth conversion between primitive and Wrapper without explicit conversion. For example, you can convert between int and Integer by simply assigning one to anther as follows:

```
public static void main(String[] args) {
        int intInput = 100;
        Integer intWrapped = null;
        int intOutput = 0;

        intWrapped = intInput; //boxing int to Integer
        intOutput = intWrapped; //boxing Integer back to int
        System.out.println(intOutput);

        double doubleInput = 200.34;
        Double doubleWrapped = null;
        double doubleOutput = 0;

        doubleWrapped = doubleInput; //boxing double to Double
        doubleOutput = doubleWrapped; //boxing Double back to double
        System.out.println(doubleOutput);


}
```

Cool, right?

ArrayList

ArrayList is just like array but only better. There are two basic different between an array and ArrayList:

1). You don't have to predefine the size of the ArrayList. It can automatically grow and shrink as needed.
2). You don't have to define the type for the elements of the ArrayList. The first element can be a number, the second one can be a string, the third one can be a boolean and so on. So ArrayList is totally heterogeneous. This turned out to be very error prone, but we have a fix for this that we will discuss in the next topic.

ArrayList has an add() method to add items to it. It has a size() method to check the current size which can freely change. It has a get() method to get and item from any index.

ArrayList is one area of Java where it is fully object-oriented. What I mean by that is that ArrayList only accepts objects and does not allow any primitive. You might think the solution to add primitive is to use the wrapper classes to convert primitives to objects, but we even have a better solution – "Boxing". Thanks to auto-boxing, introduced in Java 1.5, we can add a primitive to an ArrayList and it will automatically get converted to the corresponding wrapper object. When we take it out from ArrayList and save it to a primitive, you still have to cast it but the wrapper object again will automatically get converted to primitive. Here is an example:

```
import java.util.ArrayList;


public class ArrayListTester {
    public static void main(String[] args) {
        ArrayList aList = new ArrayList();
        aList.add(5); //auto-boxing to Integer
        aList.add(23.56); //auto-boxing to Double
        aList.add("Hello");
        for (int i=0;i<aList.size();i++){
                Object wrapped = aList.get(i);
                System.out.println(wrapped + " of type : " +
wrapped.getClass().getName());
```

```
        }
        int a = (int) aList.get(0); // auto-boxing to int from Integer
        double d = (double) aList.get(1); // auto-boxing to double from Double
        System.out.println(a);
        System.out.println(d);
    }

}
```

Here is the output:

```
5 of type : java.lang.Integer
23.56 of type : java.lang.Double
Hello of type : java.lang.String
5
23.56
```

Notice the primitives got converted to wrapper objects automatically and the opposite too happen with a little help.

Generics

As you have seen above, an ArrayList is flexible enough to allow you to put different types of data all mixed up in it. This could potentially lead to error prone code. Is there any way to stop it? Yes, generics does exactly that.

Here is an example:

```
ArrayList<Integer> aList = new ArrayList<Integer>();
```

We now created an ArrayList that only allows Integer objects. Thanks to boxing, wherever we can use Integer we can use int as well, and no casting is needed. Here is an example::

```
import java.util.ArrayList;

public class GenericsTester {
```

```
        public static void main(String[] args) {
                ArrayList<Integer> aList = new ArrayList<Integer>();
                aList.add(5); //auto-boxing to Integer
                //aList.add(23.56); // this does not compile any more, 23.56 is not int
                //aList.add("Hello"); // this does not compile either, String is not
int
                aList.add(67); // auto-boxing
                for (int i=0;i<aList.size();i++){
                        Object wrapped = aList.get(i);
                        System.out.println(wrapped + " of type : " +
wrapped.getClass().getName());
                }
                int a = aList.get(0); // auto-boxing to int from Integer and no
casting needed
                int b = aList.get(1); // auto-boxing to int from Integer and no
casting needed
                System.out.println(a);
                System.out.println(b);
        }


}
```

Here is the output:

```
5 of type : java.lang.Integer

67 of type : java.lang.Integer

5

67
```

Garbage Collection

In Java, local variables are automatically removed from the stack as soon as a method finishes execution. Static variables are in static memory and they hang out pretty much the entire time the JVM is running. So, we are left with objects in heap. What happens to objects in heap? In other programming language the programmer must carefully clean the heap objects otherwise there is be a "memory leak". Fortunately, in Java, thanks to garbage collection, unused objects in heap are automatically cleaned up by JVM.

Garbage collection is the new and innovative way of cleaning up heap in a programming language and JVM depends on it. Few questions come to mind about garbage collection:

How does Java know when to do a garbage collection?

How does Java figure out that it is OK to kill the object in the heap and return the memory back for future use? Please keep in mind that each object can have multiple references, and it is important that we don't recycle the heap space occupied by an object until all the references to the object are dead.

A simple approach would be, when we allocate an object on the heap, Java creates the object and saves room for the reference count. This count is automatically incremented every time the object is assigned to a reference. Whenever a reference goes out of scope, the reference count of the object is decremented. So, ultimately orphan objects would have a reference count of zero. The garbage collector collects all objects with zero count. However, in reality garbage collection is much more complicated, but it works very well.

How often does Java perform garbage collection?

Java performs garbage collection under the following circumstances:

a). Whenever it needs to. When the amount of memory remaining in the heap falls below a certain level, the program stops and performs garbage collection to regain whatever memory it can.
b). Whenever you ask. You can force garbage collection by calling System.gc(). Although, programmers rarely do so.
c). Whenever it gets around to it. Java continually executes a background task that looks for things to throw away. This task is low priority so as not to affect the performance of the system; however, Java will eventually get around to picking up any discarded objects left lying around.

Chapter 7

Inheritance

In the real world, an object can receive (inherit) the properties of its parent object.

If we ask someone to describe Parrot, the response would be something like "A Parrot is a beautiful bird but noisy".

Humans are great organizers. They build gigantic taxonomies to describe the relationship of one type of object to another. Organization helps us drastically reduce the amount of information we must store. For example, if you already know what a "bird" is, "A Parrot is a beautiful bird but noisy" carries a huge amount of information about Parrot.

Most of the information we know about Bird can be stored and learned in one place and reused in the classes Parrot, Geese, Sparrows and so on.

There is in fact another benefit of organizing objects in this fashion. A Parrot can be used whenever a Bird is indicated. For example, if you are asked to give an example of a Bird, you can easily present Parrot as an example. If your friend asks you to show him your pet bird, you can bring your pet Parrot.

The relationship between a Parrot and a Bird is called an IS_A relationship – A Parrot is a Bird. This relationship and its implications are fundamental to object-oriented programming.

However, it is probably worth mentioning here that the reverse is not true. A Bird is not necessarily a Parrot, and there are many other types of birds that are not Parrot.

In object-oriented programming like Java, a class can inherit fields (attributes) and methods (behaviors) from another class using the "extends" keyword.

Here is an example:

```
public class SavingsAccount extends BankAccount{
}
```

The class SavingsAccount is a new class that inherits from BankAccount class. Now, the SavingsAccount will automatically inherit all the fields and methods of BankAccount. In object-oriented programming we say that BankAccount is a super-class or base class or parent class and SavingsAccount is a sub-class or derived class or child class.

Since SavingsAccount IS_A BankAccount, we can write code like:

```
SavingsAccount sa = new SavingsAccount();
sa.deposit(500);
System.out.println(sa.getAccountNumber()); //prints 1
System.out.println(sa.getBalance()); //prints 500
```

SavingsAccount works even though the SavingsAccount looks like an *empty* class. It works because it inherited everything (for example, the deposit() method) from BankAccount. Not only that, since SavingsAccount IS_A BankAccount, we can even write code like this:

```
BankAccount b = new SavingsAccount(); //parent expected, child presented
System.out.println(b.getAccountNumber()); //prints 2
System.out.println(b.getBalance()); //prints 0
```

Notice that the left-hand side of equals sign does not match the right-hand side. We have BankAccount type on the left-hand but SavingsAccount() constructor call on the right-hand side. This is ok, since left-hand expects a parent object and the right-hand presents a child object.

Extending and Enhancing a Class

It is nice to know that a sub-class inherits fields and methods of the super-class, but if that's all it does then why should we bother to create a sub-class? There is certainly one thing we could do in the sub-class, we could add additional fields and methods so that the sub-class can do more than the super-class. For example, BankAccount may have a sub-class CheckingAccount that has an additional field to keep track of the last printed check number on check books and a couple of methods to change and retrieve this information as follows:

```java
public class CheckingAccount extends BankAccount{
    private int lastCheckNumber=0;

    public void requestChecks(int howManyChecks){
        if (howManyChecks>0){
            //some logic to print new checkbook goes here
            lastCheckNumber = lastCheckNumber + howManyChecks;
        }
    }

    public int getLastCheckNumber(){
        return lastCheckNumber;
    }
}
```

Here is a tester:

```java
public class CheckingAccountTester {
    public static void main(String[] args) {
        CheckingAccount ca = new CheckingAccount();
        ca.deposit(100);
        ca.withdrawal(50);
        ca.requestChecks(20);
        System.out.println("Account Number: " + ca.getAccountNumber()); // prints 1
        System.out.println("Last Check Number: " + ca.getLastCheckNumber()); // prints 20
        System.out.println("Balance: " + ca.getBalance()); // prints 50.0
    }
}
```

Method Hiding

Consider the following code:

```
BankAccount ca = new CheckingAccount();
ca.getLastCheckNumber(); // does not compile
```

The second line does not even compile? Why? You clearly have created a CheckingAccount object and that object certainly has the method. Then why does it not compile? Because the compiler is dumb by design. The complier looks at the variable type and finds that it is of type BankAccount. Furthermore, it finds that BankAccount has no such method, so it stops and refuses to compile.

Is there a way out of this? Sure, you can cast the variable "ca" to a CheckingAccount variable and then call the getLastCheckNumber() method on that variable and everything will be fine as follows:

```
BankAccount ca = new CheckingAccount();
CheckingAccount ca2 = (CheckingAccount) ca; // casting
ca2.getLastCheckNumber(); // compiles fine
```

Overriding

The main power of inheritance comes from the fact that a sub-class can override the method in the super-class. To override a method is to replace an inherited method with a new code so the method acts differently than the super-class. For example, in CheckingAccount class, we might need to have a boolean field for account maintenance charge and the withdrawal method in CheckingAccount might need to set it to true if the balance drops below $2000.

We can implement this new withdrawal method by adding an account maintenance charge field and overriding (I call it overwriting) the withdrawal method in CheckingAccount class. We should also add a getter to check the maintenance flag.

super. (not a typo – yes, super with a dot)

While overriding a method declared in a super-class, we may realize that the method should do exactly what the super-class's method does, plus some extra work. In our CheckingAccount example, the withdrawal method should do exactly what the withdrawal method in BankAccount does. In addition, it will check the after-withdrawal balance of the account, and if it is below 2000, it must set the account maintenance flag to true. The new withdrawal method in CheckingAccount should be able to call the withdrawal method in BankAccount class. But how? The answer is the keyword "super.". A sub-class can call any method of its super-class by using the keyword super followed by a dot.

In other words, a sub-class can call any method is super-class by using the syntax:

`super.<MethodName>`

The keyword super is very similar to the keyword this. Here is our CheckingAccount:

```java
public class CheckingAccount extends BankAccount{
        public static final double MINIMUM_BALANCE= 2000;
        private boolean maintenanceFlag=false;
        private int lastCheckNumber=0;

        public void withdrawal(double anyAmount){
                super.withdrawal(anyAmount);
                double currentBalance=getBalance();
                if (currentBalance < MINIMUM_BALANCE){
                    maintenanceFlag=true;
                }
        }

        public boolean isMaintenanceFlag() {
                return maintenanceFlag;
        }

        public void requestChecks(int howManyChecks){
                if (howManyChecks>0){
                        //some logic to print new checkbook goes here
```

```
                    lastCheckNumber = lastCheckNumber + howManyChecks;
            }
    }


    public int getLastCheckNumber(){
            return lastCheckNumber;
    }
}
```

The withdrawal method of CheckingAccount simply calls the withdrawal method at the super-class BankAccount. Then it needs to check the balance. Please keep in mind that the CheckingAccount class has no access to the private balance field of BankAccount since balance field is private in BankAccount class. So, how does CheckingAccount check the balance? Just like anybody else, by calling the public getBalance() method of BankAccount.

Notice, the getBalance() method does not have a super prefix, like super.getBalance(). Why? Because the getBalance() method is inherited as is in the CheckingAccount class (even though we don't physically see a getBalance() method in this class). However, super.getBalance() would have also worked just fine since getBalance() is certainly a method of BankAccount.

In the above example, what would have happened if the call was just withdrawal(), as opposed to super.withdrawal()? Well, it would have created an infinite recursive call to the withdrawal() method itself. Something that you certainly did not intend to do.

Hiding Fields

Fields are normally declared private – therefore, the question of overriding does not arise. Therefore, fields cannot be overridden, even public fields; they can only be hidden. If you declare a field in your sub-class that has the exact same name as a public field in your super-class, the super-class public field still exists but it can no longer be accessed directly by its name. You must use the super keyword (for example, super.fieldname) to access it.

Declaring the same field in sub-class that already exists in super-class is considered bad practice and causes all kinds of confusion. Please avoid doing so.

Constructors in a Sub-class

When we sub-class a class, all functions are inherited, all fields are inherited, the only members that are not inherited by the sub-class are the constructors. Constructors are very personal to classes and are not inherited by the sub-class – let's be very clear about it. One visual clue that constructors will not be inherited is the fact that the name of the constructor is the same as the name of the class. If constructor were really inherited, then it must change its name in the sub-class which is little too much to expect.

Anyway, this brings a very interesting dilemma. If constructors are not inherited, then how did the following code work?

```
CheckingAccount ca = new CheckingAccount();
```

After all, we didn't declare such constructor in CheckingAccount. You might recall that if a class does not declare a constructor then one default no-argument constructor is provided to the class. That explains where the constructor for CheckingAccount is coming from. However, after constructing the checking account if you execute the following code:

```
System.out.println(ca.getAccountNumber());
```

You will get a number like 1 or 2. Where is this account number coming from? That code of assigning automatic account number is in BankAccount constructor. How come that is working for CheckingAccount's default constructor? We will answer that question next.

super()

Constructors of the super-class can be called from the constructors of the sub-class. Just like the keyword this() – that refers to another constructor of the same class, the keyword super() can be used in a sub-class to call a constructor of the super-class. If you call the constructor of the super-class using the keyword super(), it must appear as the first statement in the body of a constructor; otherwise, your code will not compile.

If the super class has multiple constructors, sub-class can call any of them by passing the appropriate set of parameters. However, you can only call one of the many super constructors, so choose wisely.

Implied super() call

Calling super constructor is not really optional. Constructor of a sub-class must call one of the constructors of the super class. If you forget to make this explicit super constructor call, an implicit no-argument super() call will be embedded in your sub-class Constructor.

That's exactly is what is happening to our CheckingAccount class. We didn't write a constructor, so a default constructor is provided and in this default constructor a super() call is embedded.

In other words, our CheckingAccount has a hidden constructor provided by Java and that constructor code looks like this:

```
public CheckingAccount(){
        super();
}
```

Now that you know this, it might be a good idea to add the super() call by hand as the first line on every sub constructor you write by hand. That gives visibility of what really is going to happen when the sub constructor is executed.

Polymorphism

The word "Polymorphism" is a mouthful and it means – in layman's term – "multiple faces". Even with such a simple meaning, understanding the term in Java is difficult. Perhaps, if we start with an example, it may be helpful.

Consider a super class Shape as follows:

```
public class Shape {
        public void draw(){
                System.out.println("inside draw Shape");
        }
}
```

Now, consider two sub-classes of Shape as Circle and Square as follows:

```java
public class Circle extends Shape{
    public void draw() {
        System.out.println("Inside draw Circle");
    }
}


public class Square extends Shape{
    public void draw() {
        System.out.println("Inside draw Square");
    }
}
```

So far there is no sign of Polymorphism. Now, consider a tester class ShapeTester that has the following drawShape() method:

```java
public static void drawShape(Shape anyShape){
    anyShape.draw();
}
```

drawShape() method is extremely simple. It receives any Shape object and calls draw() method on it. From Inheritance rule we know "when a parent is expected a child can be presented". Which essentially mean, drawShape() can be called correctly by passing ether Shape (parent) or Circle (child) or Square(child). That's exactly what we will do from the main() method of ShapeTester. Here it is:

```java
public class ShapeTester {
    public static void main(String[] args) {
        Shape s = new Shape();
        Circle c = new Circle();
        Square q = new Square();
        drawShape(s);
        drawShape(c);
        drawShape(q);
```

```
        }
        public static void drawShape(Shape anyShape){
                anyShape.draw();
        }
}
```

What is the output? There are two possibilities:

1). Since drawShape is calling draw() method on Shape, each time it will print "Inside draw Shape"
2). Since we are passing 3 different shapes, each time it will print the corresponding output from the draw method.

Which one will happen? Here is the output:

```
inside draw Shape
Inside draw Circle
Inside draw Square
```

Obviously #2 happened. Why? Because, at runtime Java figures out that there is an overridden draw() method on each child class and it calls the overridden method.

Now, notice that the same drawShape() method produced three distinct output based on the type of object that is passed to it. Therefore, drawShape() method has "multiple faces", it is a Polymorphic method.

Polymorphism is also known as "Dynamic Dispatching". At runtime, the JVM dispatches the method call to the appropriate overridden method call, hence, Dynamic Dispatching occurs.

Remember two things:

a). To exhibit polymorphic behavior there must be parent-child relationship between classes. In other words, inheritance is a must for polymorphic behavior.

b). Polymorphic behavior is only observed when a method is overridden. In other words, overriding is a must for polymorphic behavior.

Final Method

Just like fields in a class, a method can also be marked as final. However, the meaning of final method is very different from the meaning of final field. A final method can't be overridden in a sub-class. It is literally the final version of the method.

While overriding a method from a super-class, the sub-class can mark the method as final – which simply means that the method can no longer be overridden.

Final Class

Just like fields and methods, a class can also be declared as a final class so that it can't be extended or sub-classed. All the fields and methods inside a final class are implicitly final (you don't have to declare them as final) because if you can't sub-class a class, how can you override any of its methods or override the value of a field? The String class, the StringBuilder class, the Math class are examples of Final classes.

While sub-classing a super-class – the sub-class can be marked as final – which simply means that the sub-class cannot be sub-classed any further.

The Object Class

We know a class can be a sub-class of another class by using the extends keyword. What happens when a class does not use any extends keyword? For example, our BankAccount class, Employee class, etc. As it turns out, classes that do not explicitly inherit from another class (like our BankAccount class, Employee class) implicitly inherit from the Object class. By that virtue, Object class is the ultimate ancestor – every class in Java extends Object either as parent or grand-parent or something else up on the chain. Therefore, Object is the ultimate Super Class in Java – a God Class if you will. Because every class in Java extends Object directly or indirectly, it is important that we study the Object Class.

The Object class has a no-argument constructor.

The Object class has the following interesting methods that are inherited by all objects:

Clone()	protected Object	Creates and returns a copy (clone) of this object. However, the clone method can't be used readily without some work on your part.
equals(Object obj)	boolean	Indicates whether some other object is "equal to" this one. By default, this method returns true if and only if both object variables are referring to the same object. In other words, it works just like "==" comparison. This method is overridden in most classes. For example, the String class has overridden this method so that the equals method compares the String content not their references.
getClass()	Class	Returns the class of an object. This method provides extremely useful information about the class of an object. This feature is known an Reflection.
toString()	String	Returns a string representation of the object. By default, the toString() method returns a string consisting of the name of the class, the at-sign character `@', and hash code of the object. This method is commonly overridden in every class to provide some meaningful information.

The toString() Method is Special (Default)

The toString() method. Inherited by every class from Object, is special – the toString() method works like a default method in many cases. Consider the following example:

```
BankAccount citiBankAccount = new BankAccount();
String s = "Bank Account: " + citiBankAccount;
System.out.println(s);
```

What would s print? We are concatenating a String with a BankAccount object. Does that even compile? How?

Turns out it compiles. It even runs and it prints "Bank Account: BankAccount@111f71" (basically classname@hashcode). How come? Java automatically calls the toString() method on citiBankAccount to convert the object to String before giving it to the println() method of System.out.

In other words, toString() method is special and used as default method in many instances.

The getClass() Method

If we have an object but don't know what class it came from, is there a way to figure out which class it came from? Yes, there is. The getClass() method, available in every object and inherited from Object class, returns the class of an object variable. For example:

```
BankAccount b = new BnakAccount();
Class clsAccount = b.getClass();
```

Now the reference variable clsAccount has all the information of BankAccount Class.

We will see the details of Class next.

The Class whose name is also Class

We already know, there is a Class in Java whose name is Object and it is the super-class of all classes. Now, I will introduce a class, whose name is also Class – uppercase C. Instances of the class "Class" represent all the classes and interfaces in a running Java application. The getName() method of this class is most often called to find out the name of the class of an object variable.

In our previous example, if we call b.getClass() it will return us an object of type Class. After that, if we call the getName() method we will get "BankAccount" as follows:

```
BankAccount b = new BankAccount();
```

```
Class clsAccount = b.getClass();
System.out.println(clsAccount.getName()); //prints BankAccount
```

Class has the following interesting methods:

getName()	String	Returns the fully qualified name of the entity (class, interface, array class, primitive type, or void) like "java.lang.String" represented by this Class object, as a String.
forName(String className)	static Class	Attempts to locate, load, link and initialize the class or interface and returns the Class object associated with the class or interface whose full pathname is given as a string. For example: Class clsString=Class.forName("java.lang.String") Now clsStirng object has the information about String class.
getDeclaredConstructors()	Constructor[]	Returns an array of Constructor objects reflecting all the constructors declared by the class represented by this Class object.
getDeclaredFields()	Field[]	Returns an array of Field objects reflecting all the fields declared by the class or interface represented by this Class object.
getDeclaredMethods()	Method[]	Returns an array of Method objects reflecting all the methods declared by the class or interface represented by this Class object.
getInterfaces()	Class[]	Determines the interfaces implemented by the class or interface represented by this object.

getModifiers()	Int	Returns the Java language modifiers for this class or interface, encoded in an integer.
getPackage()	Package	Gets the package for this class.
getSuper-class()	Class	Returns the Class representing the super-class of the entity (class, interface, primitive type or void) represented by this Class.

Chapter 8

Abstract Class

It is not uncommon in our zeal for organization to arrive at classes that do not actually represent objects. Consider the class "Bird", for example. There is no single bird on earth that is not a member of some sub-class of Bird. That is, every Bird is a Parrot or Goose or Sparrow or whatever. A class like Bird represents more of an abstract concept than a precise physical object that we can point at. Such a class is called an abstract class. In Java, an abstract class cannot be instantiated. That would make sense if we consider the following: "There are no generic birds – only specific kinds of birds. Thus, there is no instance of class Bird, only instances of sub-classes of Bird". It's not that the concept of Bird is not useful. Abstract classes represent useful generalizations of concepts.

Suppose that at our bank, the term BankAccount is really a concept. You cannot really walk into a Bank and open a BankAccount. You must open an account of one of its sub-classes like checking, savings or CD.

So, we will convert our BankAccount to an abstract class as follows:

```
public abstract class BankAccount
```

Abstract Method

Let's now assume, all sub-classes of BankAccount require a method for the calculation of interest. The trouble is, interest calculation is completely different for each sub-class of BankAccount. In this situation, it is impossible to define a calculateInterest() method for BankAccount. We can certainly define the calculateInterest() method for Checking, Savings and CD but there is nothing common between these different interest calculation logics that can be inherited from BankAccount.

However, the bank wants to enforce the policy that every sub-class of BankAccount has calculateInterest() method. We can enforce such policy in BankAccount class by declaring calculateInterest() method in BankAccount as abstract method.

An abstract method has no body. It is declared as method name followed by semicolon as follows:

```
public abstract double calculateAnnualInterest();
```

Here is another rule in Java, if a class has at least one abstract method, the class must also be an abstract class. Here is our abstract BankAccount class:

```
public abstract class BankAccount{

        private static int nextAccountNumber=1; // class level fields to autogenerate
account numbers
        private int accountNumber=0;
        private double balance=0;
        private double interestRate=0;
        private static final double defaultInterestRate=2;

        public abstract double calculateAnnualInterest();

        public static int getObjectCount(){
                return nextAccountNumber-1; //nextAccountNumber is 1 bigger
        }


        public BankAccount(){ //constructor with NO input parameter
                accountNumber=nextAccountNumber++; // assign account number
sequencially
        }
        public BankAccount(double anyBalance){//constructor with one input parameter
                // call the first constructor
                this();
                // call the deposit function to put the money in
                deposit(anyBalance);
        }

        public int getAccountNumber() {
                return accountNumber;
```

```
        }

    public void deposit(double anyAmount){
        if (anyAmount>=0){ //only positive deposit is allowed
            balance = balance + anyAmount; // balance will always be positive
        }
    }
    public void withdrawal(double anyAmount){
        if (anyAmount>=0 && anyAmount<=balance){ // can only withdraw if you
enough balance
            balance = balance - anyAmount; // balance can be zero or
positive but never negative
        }
    }

    public double getBalance() {
        return balance;
    }

    public void setInterestRate(double anyInterestRate) {
        interestRate = anyInterestRate;
    }

    public double setInterestRate() {
        interestRate = defaultInterestRate;
        return interestRate;
    }
    public double getInterestRate() {
        return interestRate;
    }
}
```

Declaring a class abstract means that the class cannot be instantiated. The following code does not compile anymore:

```
BankAccount b = new BankAccount(); //does not compile any more
```

A class that extends an abstract super-class must override every abstract method of the super-class so that it becomes a non-abstract class; otherwise the sub-class should be abstract as well. For that reason, our SavingsAccount, CheckingAccount class would not compile anymore. To make them compile again, we have two options:

a). Make SavingsAccount and CheckingAccount abstract as well
b). Implement calculateAnnualInterest() method in them

For CheckingAccount, we will take option b) and implement the method as follows:

```java
public class CheckingAccount extends BankAccount{
    public static final double MINIMUM_BALANCE= 2000;
    private boolean maintenanceFlag=false;
    private int lastCheckNumber=0;

    public double calculateAnnualInterest() {
        return getBalance()*getInterestRate();
    }

    public void withdrawal(double anyAmount){
        super.withdrawal(anyAmount);
        double currentBalance=getBalance();
        if (currentBalance < MINIMUM_BALANCE){
            maintenanceFlag=true;
        }
    }

    public boolean isMaintenanceFlag() {
        return maintenanceFlag;
    }

    public void requestChecks(int howManyChecks){
        if (howManyChecks>0){
            //some logic to print new checkbook goes here
            lastCheckNumber = lastCheckNumber + howManyChecks;
        }
    }

    public int getLastCheckNumber(){
```

```
                        return lastCheckNumber;
        }
}
```

You could have as many non-abstract methods as you wish in an abstract class. For example, deposit(), getBalance() etc. methods can be implemented right away in the abstract class BankAccount because we already know how to implement them. In other words, if you have an abstract class where you cannot implement certain methods you leave those methods as abstract. All other methods could be non-abstract methods even though the class itself is abstract.

If you want, you can sub-class a non-abstract class, add one or more new abstract methods and make the sub-class as abstract.

It is also possible to make a class abstract where the class has no abstract method at all. This is perfectly allowed in Java.

Constructors of Abstract Class

An abstract class cannot be instantiated – period. There is no way to create object from an abstract class. If that's the case, why would you even bother writing constructors for an abstract class? After all, constructors are needed for object creation and that very object creation is prohibited for abstract classes. The answer is, for the child classes so that they can make super() call. Think of this way, if you never plan to go back to college, why would you save money for college tuition? The answer is, for the children.

Interface

Java supports a concept like class, called the interface. An interface is a collection of abstract methods. All methods within an interface are implicitly public and abstract. Fields within an interface, if they exist at all, are implicitly final, public and static (in other words, they are constants). From Java 8, interface can have static methods and default method etc. but we will stick to the basic interface definition for now.

Imagine you are writing an application for a rental company. This company rents cars, furniture, electronics to name a few. Therefore, there is an abstract class Car, another abstract class Furniture and another abstract class Electronics and so on. There is no common super class to these abstract classes other than Object class. However, the all of them should have a setRent() and getRent() method. Where do you define these methods? If you define them in Car, then all sub-classes of Car will inherit them, but Furniture and Electronics sub-classes will not. Therefore, it would be good idea to define these two methods someplace else and incorporate them in all classes. The way to do that is to define an interface like Rentable as follows:

```
public interface Rentable {
        public abstract void setRent(double anyRent);
        public abstract double getRent();
}
```

Notice I have added public and abstract before the two method names. That is for clarity. Even if I forget to add those two keywords, these methods would still be abstract and public.

An interface allows the programmer to describe a set of capabilities that a collection of heterogeneous classes might be interested in implementing. A class inherits the methods of an interface using "implements" keyword. Here is an example:

```
public abstract class Car implements Rentable {
}
```

Now, the Car class has two abstract methods inherited from Rentable.

A Furniture class can also inherit the same two abstract methods as follows:

```
public abstract class Furniture implements Rentable{
}
```

Both Car and Furniture class got away without implementing the setRent() and getRent() method because they are abstract classes and abstract classes can have or can inherit abstract methods without a problem. A sub-class of Car that is not abstract can't get away without implementing those two methods. Here is an example of Sedan:

```
public class Sedan extends Car{
      private double rent;

      public void setRent(double anyRent) {
            rent = anyRent;
      }

      public double getRent() {
            return rent;
      }
}
```

In Java, you can only extend from one super-class. In other words, Java does not support multiple inheritance, but you can certainly implement more than one interface by adding them in a comma separated list. Imagine our rental company also has another interface Discountable that contains setDiscountRate() and getDiscountRate() that all Electronics item must also implement in addition to Rentable. Here is the interface:

```
public interface Discountable {
      public abstract void setDiscountRate(double anyDiscount);
      public abstract double getDiscountRate();
}
```

In that case our Electronics class would look like this:

```
public abstract class Electronics implements Rentable, Discountable {
}
```

Notice the comma separates list of interfaces.

Inheritance between Interfaces

It is quite reasonable to think that we need an interface that inherits all abstract methods from another interface and then adds some.

Here an example of an super interface if you will:

```
public interface Sport {
        public abstract void setHomeTeamName(String name);
        public abstract void setVisitingTeamName(String name);
        public abstract String getHomeTeamName();
        public abstract String getVisitingTeamName();
}
```

Then we could have another interface that inherits all these abstract methods and adds a few more:

```
public interface Hokey extends Sport {
        public abstract void addHomeGoal();
        public abstract void addVisitingGoal();

        public abstract void homeGoalScored();
        public abstract void visitingGoalScored();
}
```

Now Hokey inherits all the abstract methods from Sport.

Enumeration

Suppose you want to represent the days of a week in a program. You could you the integers 0,1,2 etc. to represent the days but that would not be very solid since "int" is not limited to just 0 through 6.

You can use enum keyword to create an enumeration type whose values are limited to a set of symbolic names.

Here is our enum for days of a week.

```
enum WeekDays {
Sunday,
Monday,
Tuesday,
Wednesday,
```

```
Thursday,
Friday,
Saturday
}
```

In this enumeration, Sunday is 0, Monday is 1, Tuesday is 2, Wednesday is 3 and so forth. Enums have name() method to get back their name and ordinal() method to get back their number. Here is an example:

```
public class WeekDayTester {
        public static void main(String[] args) {
                WeekDays today = null;
                today = WeekDays.Wednesday;
                System.out.println(today.name()); //prints Wednesday
                System.out.println(today.ordinal()); // prints 3


        }
}
```

Sometimes you need to enumerate discrete values like nickel=5, dime=10 and so on.

To do that, you need to define a constructor for the enum. Funny thing is you can never call the constructor; therefore, you are better off defining the constructor as private.

On a separate note, you can add methods in a enum as well. It seems like having a value() method that returns the int value of a coin is a great idea since the ordinal is useless.

Here it is:

```
public enum Coin {
        Penny(1),Nickel(5),Dime(10),Quarter(25);
        private int coinValue;

        private Coin(int anyValue){
                coinValue=anyValue;
        }
        public int value(){
```

```
            return coinValue;
        }
}
```

Here is the tester:

```
public class CoinTester {
    public static void main(String[] args) {
        Coin n = Coin.Nickel;
        System.out.println(n.name()); // Nickel
        System.out.println(n.value()); //5
        System.out.println(n.ordinal()); //1
    }
}
```

Packages

Packaging in Java is a way to group a collection of classes together. Java uses packages to:

a). Uniquely identify a class.
b). Store a collection of related class files, that are not only physically located in a directory but are also tied together as part of one group.

A package in Java is:

a). A physical directory on the file system
b). A library of classes
c). Together with the class name, a unique identifier for a class.

Let's go ahead and create a package in Java using Eclipse. Right click on your project, Select New→Package. Type "edu.nyu.myPackage" as Name of the Package and click Finish.

You will see, under src folder of your project, there is a package created under the same name.

Now, select your package and right click and select New→Class. Type "PackagedClass" as the name of the class and click Finish. You will see your class is now created under the package. Double click on the class name to open the source code, you will see the following:

```
package edu.nyu.mypackage;
public class PackagedClass {


}
```

Notice the first line: `package edu.nyu.mypackage;`

That's new. That's saying this class is in this package. Try to create another Class in the same package using the same name. You will notice that the Finish button is disabled and up top there is the following message "Type already exists." If you try to create the same class outside of the package you will have no problem. Which means, class names are not guaranteed to be unique, but class names combined with package name must be unique.

Now right click on the package name and select Properties. You will see a location of the package. In my case I see:

C:\Users\rahmanm\workspace\CCJChapter8\src\edu\nyu\mypackage

If you copy this location in explorer you will land on a folder named "mypackage" which is under "nyu" folder, which in turn is under "edu" folder. So, a package in Java is a physical folder and each dot in the package name translates to a corresponding sub folder.

Let's create a second class in the package named PackagedClassTester and check off the main method. Add few lines of code in the main method as follows:

```
package edu.nyu.mypackage;
public class PackagedClassTester {
        public static void main(String[] args) {
                PackagedClass pc = new PackagedClass();
                Class c = pc.getClass();
```

```
        System.out.println(c.getName());
    }
}
```

Run the code. The output is:

```
edu.nyu.mypackage.PackagedClass
```

So, our PackagedClass is no longer just PackagedClass, it now has a prefix of edu.nyu.mypackage. Together the class has a fully qualified name "edu.nyu.mypackage.PackagedClass".

CLASSPATH

In Eclipse, you never have to worry about CLASSPATH since Eclipse automatically takes care of it but outside of Eclipse, let's say, on command prompt, if you want to run the PackagedClassTester, you must define a CLASSPATH variable in your environment settings. Your CLASSPATH must point to the root of the package where the compiled class are located. If you have many packages in various folders you will need to add those folders in your CLASSPATH (in windows a semicolon separated list, in Unix a colon separated list)

Import Statement

Let's create another package called "edu.nyu.tester". In this tester create another tester class called NewPackagedClassTester, check off the main method. Type the following code in the main() method of this tester:

```
PackagedClass pc = new PackagedClass();
```

You will be surprised to see that the code does not compile. Why? Because PackagedClass is in a different package than NewPackagedClassTester and they don't see each other. So, how do you resolve this error? There are two ways to about it:

1). You can type in the fully qualified class name in both sides as follows:

```
edu.nyu.mypackage.PackagedClass pc = new edu.nyu.mypackage.PackagedClass();
```

Notice you need to put fully qualified class name even before the constructor name.
or

2). You can right click on the red error and select import option which will add an import statement: "import edu.nyu.mypackage.PackagedClass" before the class name as follows:

```
package edu.nyu.tester;


import edu.nyu.mypackage.PackagedClass;


public class NewPackagedClassTester {
        public static void main(String[] args) {
            PackagedClass pc = new PackagedClass();
        }
}
```

You can import all the classes in a package using a wildcard statement like this:

```
import edu.nyu.mypackage.*;
```

This will import all the classes from edu.nyu.mypackage in one shot.

The word "import" is misleading. It tends to suggest that you physically importing code from other classes which is, obviously, not true. You are merely resolving the reference to a specific class or set of classes.

Implicit Import

So far, all the classes we have used like String, StringBuilder and so on are in package "java. lang" (which means the class files are located in a folder named "java\lang\"). If that's true, it is surprising that our code worked without an import statement as follows:

```
import java.lang.*;
```

Because we cannot do anything without the core package "java.lang", Java implicitly adds the import statement to all the classes we create, so that we don't have to explicitly write this import statement in every class.

Default Nameless Package

In Java, every class must be in a package. If that's true, how did we get away without a package statement so far? Here is the answer. If a class has no package statement, the class is added to a default nameless package. All our classes we have created so far are, in fact, in this default nameless package and Eclipse even says so. Go back to your projects src folder and you will see "(default package)" and all your unpackaged classes are in there.

Import is only needed for other packages

Classes of the same package see each other just fine. You don't need to import classes of the same package. Import is required for classes outside the package.

Package Naming

Please keep in mind that one of the key importance of package is that together with the class name, the class becomes uniquely identifiable. Therefore, a package name should prevent collisions with other packages, so choosing a name that's both meaningful and unique is an import aspect of package design. But programmers around the globe are developing packages and classes all the time so there is no way to find out who is using what package names and no way to keep this uniqueness intact. A good way to ensure unique package names is to use the Internet domain name of your company. If you are working for a sales application for a company named Global Inc. that owns the domain name global.com, then a package declaration within sales application may look like:

```
package com.global.sales.invoice;
```

Notice that the components of the domain name are reversed from the normal domain name convention (for example: com.global instead of global.com), that makes the sorting of the package names easier on your hard disk and development tool.

If you use this convention, your package names should not conflict with those of anyone else, except possibly within your organization. If such conflicts arise, you can further qualify by adding a more specific department name, application name etc. as we did above.

JAR File

A JAR file (stands for Java Archive) is nothing but a zip file that can be used to store a collection of classes in a number of packages all as one unit. A JAR file allows ease of distribution of your code. Eclipse makes JAR file creation piece of cake. Right click on your project. Select Export→JAR file. Select a name and location of your JAR and you are done.

If you want to see the content of the jar file, here is an easy way:

 a). Navigate to the folder where you created the jar file.
 b). Right click on the file, select Rename, change the extension of the file from jar to zip
 c). Now double click on the file to use WinZip to open the file.
 d). You should see all the classes in all the packages are stored in the jar file.

You could now distribute your complied application as JAR file to others.

Visibility - Protected Fields & Methods

We know about public and private fields/methods already. With the introduction of the concept of package we need to discuss protected field & method. Declaring a field/method protected means that it is accessible to two groups of classes:

 a). Classes in the same package
 b). Sub-classes of this class irrespective of the package name of the sub-classes.

Notice that protected is less protected than private. A class can also be protected but we will skip that discussion.

Usage of protected field/method is not popular in Java. You don't have to use it often.

Visibility - Default or Friendly

If we do not specify any scope like public, protected or private to a field/method, but simply leave it blank (like we do for local variables), then that field/ method automatically gets a default or friendly scope which simply means that the field/ method is only accessible to the members of the same package. Nothing else.

Notice, default is more restrictive than protected but less restrictive than private. A class can also have default scope, but we will skip that discussion.

Usage of friendly field/method is not popular in Java. You don't have to use it often.

public	>	protected	>	default	>	private
(everyone)		(package + sub-class)		(package only)		(this class only)

Chapter 9

Exception

The exception mechanism is Java's way of detecting and reporting errors. The Throwable class is the superclass of all errors and exceptions in the Java language. Throwable has two subclasses, Error and Exception that are conventionally used to indicate that exceptional situations have occurred.

An Error is a subclass of Throwable that indicates serious problems that a reasonable application should not try to catch. On the other hand, the class Exception and its subclasses are a form of Throwable sub-classes that indicates conditions that a reasonable application might want to catch.

By convention, class Throwable and its subclasses have two constructors, one that takes no arguments and one that takes a string argument that can be used to produce an error message.

A Throwable class contains a snapshot of the execution stack of its execution thread at the time it was created. The execution stack information can be printed by calling the printStackTrace() method.

Problems with good old Error Returns

Before Exception was invented, return value from a function was used to indicate error. The theory behind using good old error return is simple: When error occurs, every function should return an error indication. In addition, every caller should check the error indications returned by the function it called and take appropriate actions.

But there are quite a few problems with this approach:

a). **Complex logic**: Returning error indication when erroneous situation occurs is not typically a problem. The problem arises, however, when the caller must check that error returned and act. Pretty soon the amount of logic devoted to checking error returns and taking actions is more than the amount of code devoted to getting the work done. Eventually, the error logic starts to obscure the main logic flow.

b). **Limited information**: A limited amount of information can be encoded in a single error return value. For example, a square() method returns -1. What does it mean? You need to consult some other documentation to get a full description of error if such documentation exists at all.

c). **Used-up returns**: An error return can get in the way of a function that returns its own non-error value. For example, if a sum() method returns -1 is that a good result or error? Could be either.

d). **No returns**: Some methods return void. Java constructors don't return any value at all. This means that there is no way to pass back an error indication from a void method or a constructor.

The Exception Alternative

Java borrows an alternative error reporting mechanism from the ADA programming language: Exceptions. The idea is simple. When an error condition occurs, execution is paused, and an object of type Exception is created. The object is then populated will all the information about the error and passed back to the error handing block of the same method or to the caller. This happens even if the method returns void or does not return anything at all (like constructors).

Throwing an Exception

Raising an error condition is done in java by using two steps:

a). Create an Exception Object as follows:
```
Exception e = new Exception("zero or negative number of items not allows.");
```

b). Use the keyword "throw" followed by the Exception object as follows:
```
throw e;
```

In practice though, these two lines are combined in one to give the following format:

```
throw new Exception("zero or negative number of items not allows.");
```

Our BankAccount class has a deposit method that looks like this:

```
public void deposit(double anyAmount){
      if (anyAmount>=0){ //only positive deposit is allowed
            balance = balance + anyAmount;
      }
}
```

Notice the method silently throw away any negative deposit. In practice, it should throw an exception in those cases. Here is our modified deposit method with exception added:

```
public void deposit(double anyAmount){
      if (anyAmount>=0){ //only positive deposit is allowed
            balance = balance + anyAmount; // balance will always be positive
      }
      else{
            throw new Exception("Negative deposit is not allowed");
      }
}
```

However, the above code does not compile. Why? I will explain next.

Unhandled Exceptions must be advertised

If a method throws Exception, the method must advertise such fact so that the caller can be prepared to handle the error condition. It is unfair for the caller not to know about potential Exceptions from the method it calls. Now the question is, how and where do we put this advertisement about exception. The only place where an advertisement for Exception can be placed and be visible to others is method declarations. That's exactly where you have reveal exceptions using the "throws" keyword as follows:

```
public void deposit(double anyAmount) throws Exception{
```

Notice, this time the keyword is "throws" not "throw".

I personally have a problem with the choice of word "throws" when it really means "may throw" but that's just the way it is.

Now the deposit() method will compile but the BankAccount class would break in the constructor. Why? I will explain next.

Ways to Handle Exception

Let's now turn our focus, for a moment, to the caller of a function with exception. The second constructor of BankAccount that receives balance as argument and calls deposit() method. This constructor does not compile anymore. We know, in Java, if a method throws exception it gives the caller an opportunity to do something about it by advertising it. The caller now, being properly notified about the potential exception, cannot simply do nothing about it. It must do something. As a matter of fact, there are two options for the caller to pick from:

a). Propagate the exception further up, otherwise known as bubbling up the Exception by saying throws in the declaration.
b). Handle the potential exception

In case of the second constructor of BankAccount, it should not handle the negative deposit since it merely received such negative value from its own caller. So, it should simply bubble up the exception by adding a throws clause in its declaration as follows:

So, the constructor would look as follows:

```
public BankAccount(double anyBalance) throws Exception{//constructor with one input
parameter
        // call the first constructor
        this();
        // call the deposit function to put the money in
        deposit(anyBalance);
}
```

Notice we added a throws clause to the declaration of the constructor even though it does not actually throw any exception in the body of the constructor. It calls deposit() method that does so. I call this "guilty by association".

Now BankAccount class does compile.

Surprisingly our CheckingAccountTester does not compile anymore. Why? Because it calls the deposit() method and deposit() method now throws Exception. What should the CheckingAccountTester do? Bubble up the exception or handle it? The answer is, CheckingAccountTester is the end of this call chain and it is the one that is sending the amount to deposit. So, it really should handle it. How? That's our next topic.

By the way, the BankAccountTester does not compile ever since we made BankAccount abstract and that's ok. That tester will never compile again since it tries to create object from BankAccount which is abstract and abstract class cannot be instantiated so should simply ignore this tester.

Catching Exception

Let's look at the CheckingAccountTester again:

```java
public class CheckingAccountTester {
    public static void main(String[] args) {
        CheckingAccount ca = new CheckingAccount();
        ca.deposit(100);
        ca.withdrawal(50);
        ca.requestChecks(20);
        System.out.println("Account Number: " + ca.getAccountNumber());
        System.out.println("Last Check Number: " + ca.getLastCheckNumber());
        System.out.println("Balance: " + ca.getBalance());
    }
}
```

Notice that the tester is sending positive $100 to the deposit method so the question of exception occurrence does not even arise here. Yet, it must handle the possibility of such exception.

Handling Exception in java is done by introducing two additional blocks: 1) try block and 2) catch block. The keyword "try" is used to introduce a "try block" . The "try block" should enclose the method call. Then, the keyword "catch" is used to introduce "catch block". The "catch block" is the error handling block, here you write error handing logic. Here is an example of such try-catch:

```java
CheckingAccount ca = new CheckingAccount();
try{
      ca.deposit(100);
}
catch(Exception anyException){
      anyException.printStackTrace();
}
ca.withdrawal(50);
ca.requestChecks(20);
System.out.println("Account Number: " + ca.getAccountNumber());
System.out.println("Last Check Number: " + ca.getLastCheckNumber());
System.out.println("Balance: " + ca.getBalance());
```

Although this works, it is recommended not to use try block in the middle of your code to wrap one method call. Instead, you should wrap all your code into one try block although rest don't throw any exception and then the catch block will follow as follows:

```java
public class CheckingAccountTester {
   public static void main(String[] args) {
      try{
            CheckingAccount ca = new CheckingAccount();
            ca.deposit(100);
            ca.withdrawal(50);
            ca.requestChecks(20);
            System.out.println("Account Number: " +
ca.getAccountNumber());
            System.out.println("Last Check Number: " + ca.getLastCheckNumber());
            System.out.println("Balance: " + ca.getBalance());
      }
      catch(Exception anyException){
            anyException.printStackTrace();
      }

   }
```

}

So, how does it work? Here is the mode of operation of try block:

a). If there is no error, the code in try block executes in sequential fashion, if the try block finished without any error, the catch block is completely skipped and the code after the catch block starts to execute in sequential fashion. Which is what will happen in this case since we are depositing positive $100.

b). The moment try block comes across exception, the control jumps from try block to catch block skipping all the following lines of the try block. The catch block then executes in sequential fashion. After the catch block is done, the code after the catch block starts to execute in sequential fashion. To so see this mode in action, simple pass negative $100 to the deposit method from the tester as follows:

```
ca.deposit(-100); //negative 100 is passed to deposit method
```

Now step through the tester one line at a time using debugging mode. You will see that the control will jump from the deposit call to the exception block indicating error.

Creating your own Exception Class

The Exception class is fine, but it does not have any fields or methods that may be needed to meet your requirements. For example, while throwing the exception from deposit() method, we may need to store the account number and balance inside the exception object as fields but the basic Exception class does not have such fields. Also, throwing and catching all exceptions as generic "Exception" violated object-oriented design. Exception class should be sub-classed to custom exception classes.

In Java, Exception class has already been sub-classed to several classes, however, you are free to define your own exception classes to fit your needs.

It will be nice if the deposit() method throws NegativeAmountException - in case of negative withdrawal. This NegativeAmountException would contain the negative amount, account number as fields and getters for them. It would also make sense that the constructor of

NegativeAmountException will have these values as input parameters. Here it is:

```java
public class NegativeAmountException extends Exception{
    private double negativeAmount=0;
    private int accountNumber=0;
    public NegativeAmountException(double anyAmount, int anyAccountNumber){
        negativeAmount=anyAmount;
        accountNumber=anyAccountNumber;
    }
    public double getNegativeAmount() {
        return negativeAmount;
    }
    public int getAccountNumber() {
        return accountNumber;
    }
}
```

Let's go ahead and use this in BankAccount's deposit() method:

```java
public void deposit(double anyAmount) throws NegativeAmountException{
    if (anyAmount>=0){ //only positive deposit is allowed
        balance = balance + anyAmount; // balance will always be positive
    }
    else{
        throw new NegativeAmountException(anyAmount, accountNumber);
    }
}
```

Although the constructor is not complaining, we should fix it too so that in throws NegativeAmountException instead of general Exception as follows:

```java
public BankAccount(double anyBalance) throws NegativeAmountException{ //constructor
with one input parameter
        // call the first constructor
        this();
        // call the deposit function to put the money in
        deposit(anyBalance);
}
```

The CheckingAccountTester is also not complaining but we should fix it's catch block too to catch

NegativeAmountException as follows:

```
public class CheckingAccountTester {
        public static void main(String[] args) {
                try{
                    CheckingAccount ca = new CheckingAccount();
                    ca.deposit(100);
                    ca.withdrawal(50);
                    ca.requestChecks(20);
                    System.out.println("Account Number: " + ca.getAccountNumber());
                    System.out.println("Last Check Number: " +
ca.getLastCheckNumber());
                    System.out.println("Balance: " + ca.getBalance());
                }
                catch(NegativeAmountException anyException){
                    anyException.printStackTrace();
                }


        }
}
```

Creating multiple Exception Classes

Now let's focus on the withdrawal() method:

```
public void withdrawal(double anyAmount){
        if (anyAmount>=0 && anyAmount<=balance){ // can only withdraw if you enough
balance
                balance = balance - anyAmount; // balance can be zero or positive but
never negative
        }
}
```

It will be nice if the withdrawal() method also throws NegativeAmountException - in case of negative withdrawal.

Similarly, it would be great if the withdrawal() method also throws a InsufficientBalanceException when withdrawal amount is greater than the balance. This InsufficientBalanceException would contain withdrawal amount, balance and account number as fields and getters for them. It would also make sense that the constructor of InsufficientBalanceException will have these values as input parameters.

Let's go ahead and create this Exceptions first.

```java
public class InsufficientBalanceException extends Exception {
      private double balance=0;
      private double amount=0;
      private int accountNumber=0;
      public InsufficientBalanceException(double anyBalance, double anyAmount, int
anyAccountNumber){
            balance = anyBalance;
            amount = anyAmount;
            accountNumber = anyAccountNumber;
      }
      public double getBalance() {
            return balance;
      }
      public double getAmount() {
            return amount;
      }
      public int getAccountNumber() {
            return accountNumber;
      }
}
```

Throwing Multiple Exceptions

A single method can throw more than one Exception in the body of the method. When it does, it must advertise all these exception by comma separating the list of Exceptions in the throws clause of the method declaration.

Now that we have two Exceptions that can be thrown by withdrawal() method, let's throw these Exceptions in our withdrawal() method as follows:

```java
public void withdrawal(double anyAmount) throws NegativeAmountException,
```

```
InsufficientBalanceException{
     if (anyAmount<0){
          throw new NegativeAmountException(anyAmount, accountNumber);
     }
     if (anyAmount>balance){
          throw new InsufficientBalanceException(balance, anyAmount,
accountNumber);
     }
     balance = balance - anyAmount; // balance can be zero or positive but never
negative
}
```

Notice the comma-separated list of exceptions in the method declaration.

Handling Multiple Exceptions

Now the CheckingAccount 's withdrawal() method is broken since it calls the withdrawal() method on the parent class BankAccount. Since this method is an intermediate method, it should simply bubble up the exception as follows:

```
public void withdrawal(double anyAmount) throws NegativeAmountException,
InsufficientBalanceException{
     super.withdrawal(anyAmount);
     double currentBalance=getBalance();
     if (currentBalance < MINIMUM _ BALANCE){
          maintenanceFlag=true;
     }
}
```

CheckingAccount's withdrawal() method now bubbling up two exceptions as comma-separated list.

Now CheckingAccountTester is broken again since it only handles NegativeAmountException but not InsufficientBalanceException. Let's fix it too:

```
public class CheckingAccountTester {
     public static void main(String[] args) {
          try{
               CheckingAccount ca = new CheckingAccount();
```

```
            ca.deposit(100);
            ca.withdrawal(50);
            ca.requestChecks(20);
            System.out.println("Account Number: " + ca.getAccountNumber());
            System.out.println("Last Check Number: " +
ca.getLastCheckNumber());
            System.out.println("Balance: " + ca.getBalance());
        }
        catch(NegativeAmountException anyException){
            anyException.printStackTrace();
        } catch (InsufficientBalanceException anotherException) {
            anotherException.printStackTrace();
        }
    }
}
```

Notice we have two catch blocks now – each one handing one type of exception. You can have as many catch blocks as you need. There is no limit to it.

One more thing. When you have multiple catch blocks, java compares the exception thrown with each catch block starting at the first catch block and stops at the first one that matches. Since the search of a catch block is performed in the order that the catch blocks appear, it is important to put more specific catch blocks earlier and more generic catch blocks later. Fortunately, if you do a wrong ordering of catch blocks, the compiler will warn you about the wrong order but let you compile anyway.

Finally Block

Control exits from a try block under three circumstances:

a). The end of try block is reached without any exception.
b). An exception is thrown.
c). The program executes a "return" statement before reaching the end of try block and there is no exception thrown.

Wouldn't it be nice to execute some common code before exiting under any of the three conditions mentioned above? Java allows to define a block of code to be executed before control exits the methods in any of the above three scenarios. This is called the "finally block" because it is defined using the keyword "finally". The finally block is optional but once defined there is no way to escape the execution of finally block. It will be executed in all three conditions stated above. I call the finally block the "catch all block" since it is guaranteed to execute.

The key thing to remember is that the finally block always executes no matter how you exited the try block. The "finally" block is executed before control exits the try-catch-finally block, even if the try block contains a return statement or no exception has occurred. This makes the "finally" block an ideal place to do some housekeeping like release resources that the method might have used. For example, you might close any open file in the "finally" block because they need to be closed regardless whether there was an error or not. Unfortunately, our CheckingAccountTester does not really need a finally block. But we will put one in just for fun. Here it is:

```
try{
        CheckingAccount ca = new CheckingAccount();
        ca.deposit(100);
        ca.withdrawal(50);
        ca.requestChecks(20);
        System.out.println("Account Number: " + ca.getAccountNumber());
        System.out.println("Last Check Number: " + ca.getLastCheckNumber());
        System.out.println("Balance: " + ca.getBalance());
}
catch(NegativeAmountException anyException){
        anyException.printStackTrace();
} catch (InsufficientBalanceException anotherException) {
        anotherException.printStackTrace();
}
finally{
        System.out.println("Exiting the tester");
}
```

RuntimeException – Unchecked Exception

We know that if a method throws exception, the caller must do something about it: either catch it or bubble it up. Otherwise, the code would not even compile. If that's true, how come your code was compiling fine without any knowledge of exception, when you occasionally saw for sure that your code was throwing NullPointerException, IndexOutOfBoundsException etc.? Well, there is a loop-hole. Here is the correct statement – "if a method throws exception, the caller must do something about it, unless the exception is RuntimeException or its sub-class. RuntimeException does not need a catch block".

What is RuntimeException? RuntimeException, a subclass of Exception that Java RunTime (JVM) throws. A method is not required to declare in its throws clause RuntimeException or any sub-classes of RuntimeException. Therefore, there is no need to catch them by the caller either.

Be careful though. Don't throw RuntimeException in your code. You must have a very good reason to throw a RuntimeException or create an exception that is subclass of RuntimeException since you know they are designed for the JVM to throw and they don't need to be caught.

Finally, one latest development on exceptions in Java. A lot of people are arguing that all Java exceptions should be unchecked. Forcing the caller to catch an exception is a bad design. Well, I will let you be the judge of that.

Chapter 10

Input/Output

The support for Input/Output in Java is certainly not straightforward. Java uses 2-bytes Unicode characters for data while keyboards and consoles of many operating systems still use 1-byte data. Therefore, Java is forced to support both types of data. When it comes to I/O, you will notice two sets of similar classes in Java – one for 2-bytes Unicode Data, another for 1-byte data.

Files and Streams

The way that an operating system stores data is by putting it in a file. It also retrieves data from file. The operating system even treats console as an output file and keyboard as an input file. Therefore, as far as the operating system is concerned all I/O is file I/O.

Java builds another level of abstraction on top of it. The way Java stores and retrieves data to and from a file is by connecting a stream to the data. A stream - in real life - could be supplied by a lake, by a spring and so on. Similarly, a stream - in Java - could be bytes coming from a file or going out to a file, and a file does not have to be physical file – it can be a keyboard, console, printer and so on.

In JDK 1.0, streams like InputStream, OutputStream were a flow of 1-byte data. JDK 1.1 introduced Readers and Writes that are 2-bytes Unicode character streams. Java strongly recommends that we stay away from – whenever possible - 1-byte streams and use 2-bytes Readers and Writers instead. However, you will notice that that's not always possible.

The IOException class is used by many methods related to I/O to signal exception conditions.

Internally, characters are always 2-bytes Unicode characters in Java. However, the Standard Input and Output in Java (which basically means reading from the keyboard and writing out to the console) is still 1-byte streams.

What is System.out?

You are already familiar with the System class. Specifically, System.out.println() that we use all the time. What is System.out anyway? Well, System is a class name and out does not have parenthesis next to it. So "out" is a field. Now that we know "out" is a field, it must be public static field of System class, right? Absolutely, since we are accessing this field directly by the class name. Now, what type of field is "out"? int? string? You don't know, you can't tell but there is a clue. You use System.out.println() method all the time, right? So, println() must be a method on "out" field. Therefore, "out" must be an object type field that has methods. But what type of object is "out"? That you can't tell for sure without looking. If you consult Java documentation (Also known as JavaDoc) you will see the following:

```
public static final java.io.PrintStream out;
```

So, out is of type java.io.PrintStream. What is PrintStream anyway? To find out, in your code, type the following line:

```
java.io.PrintStream p;
```

Highlight the word PrintStream, right click and select "Open Type Hierarchy" (or press F4). You will see the following screen:

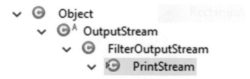

What do you learn from here? PrintStream is a subclass of FilterOutputStream. In turn, FilterOutputStream is a subclass of OutputStream and finally, of course, OutputStream is a subclass of Object – just like any other class. So, what is OutputSteam anyway you might ask. OutputStream class is the superclass of all 1-byte output related class. The OutputStream class is an abstract class because it has an abstract write(int b)method that writes the specified byte to the output stream. In our case, System.out field is using a grandchild of OutputStream called PrintStream to write to our console.

There is another PrintStream field on System class called System.err. This one is used to send errors to our console.

What is System.in?

Unknown to you, System class also have another public static final field knows an "in" as follows:

```
public static final java.io.InputStream in;
```

So, what is InputStream? InputStream class is the superclass of all 1-byte input related class. The InputStream class is an abstract class because it has an abstract read() method that reads the next byte from the input stream. In our case, System.in field is using a this InputStream to read from our keyboard.

One more thing, abstract classes cannot be instantiated (we know this already). So, the actual object that System.in points to cannot possibly be an instance of InputStream. It must be a concrete subclass of InputStream that has no abstract method. What is that sub-class? Let's find out using Reflection. Run the following code in any main() method:

```
System.out.println(System.in.getClass().getName());
```

It will print:

```
java.io.BufferedInputStream
```

So, System.in is really a BufferedInputStream which is a subclass of InputStream.

Now, let's test System.in with the following code:

```
import java.io.IOException;
public class InTester {
```

```
    public static void main(String[] args) {
        try {
            System.out.println("System.in is: " +
System.in.getClass().getName());

            System.out.print("Press any letter key and hit <Enter>: ");
            int input = System.in.read();
            System.out.println("Ascii input: " + input);
            char c = (char) input;
            System.out.println("char input: " + c);
        } catch (IOException e) {
            e.printStackTrace();
        }

    }
}
```

Run the code, mouse click on the console tab in Eclipse after the word "<Enter>:" and type any letter and hit the enter key. It will print the ascii code of the letter and then the letter itself as follows:

```
System.in is: java.io.BufferedInputStream
Press any letter key and hit <Enter>: h
Ascii input: 104
char input: h
```

If you want to read multiple characters at a time from the keyboard, that is also possible by providing an empty array of bytes to the overloaded read method. The empty array will get filled with your input data and then you can convert it to string and spit back as follows:

```
import java.io.IOException;

public class MultiCharacterInTester {
    public static void main(String[] args) {
        try {
            System.out.print("Enter few letters and hit <Enter>: ");
            byte[] inputByteArray = new byte[256];
            int characterCount = System.in.read(inputByteArray);
            System.out.println("Number of characters typed: " +
characterCount);

            String inputString = new String(inputByteArray); // convert to
```

```
String
                     System.out.println("Input: " + inputString.trim()); //remove
trailing spaces before print
             } catch (IOException e) {
                 e.printStackTrace();
             }


        }
}
```

Type a few letters and hit <Enter>. Your input length as well as your actual input will be printed as follows:

```
Enter few letters and hit <Enter>: To be or not to be
Number of characters typed: 20
Input: To be or not to be
```

Byte Streams and Character Streams

As I mentioned before, Java I/O package has two sets of classes:

a). 1-byte stream classes – known as byte stream - primary used by Java to read from standard input (keyboard) and write to standard output (console). Byte stream classes can be easily identified by the keyword "Stream" at the end of class name.

b). 2-bytes stream classes – known as Unicode character stream - used by programmers to do all other I/O. Character stream classes can be easily identified by the keyword "Reader" or "Writer" at the end of the class name.

The standard byte streams System.in, System.out, System.err existed before Unicode character streams were invented. This causes some confusion about I/O in Java.

Conversion of Input Bytes to Characters

Java internally uses characters but the input from System.in comes in as bytes. Therefore, we need to convert these bytes to characters as they come in from System.in. Fortunately, there is a class in Java called InputStreamReader (notice this class has both "Stream" and "Reader" keywords) that can convert bytes stream to the corresponding Unicode character stream.

Reading a Line

BufferedReader, a direct subclass of Reader, acts as a wrapper around a Reader, buffers input and provides readLine() method to read a complete line at a time. Therefore, by using a combination of InputStreamReader and BufferedReader to wrap System.in, we should be able to read a line at a time from the keyboard.

Conversion of Output Characters to Bytes

Java internally uses characters but output to System.out or System.err must go out as bytes. Therefore, we need to convert characters to bytes as they go out to System.out or System.err. Fortunately, there is another class in Java called OutputStreamWriter (notice this class has both "Stream" and "Writer" keywords) that can convert characters stream to the corresponding byte stream.

Writing a Line

PrintWriter, a direct subclass of Writer, acts as a wrapper around a Writer, provides println() method to write any type of data with a newline at the end. Therefore, by using a combination of OuputStreamWriter and PrintWriter to wrap System.out, we should be able to write a line at a time.

Here is an example of wrapping both System.in and System.out by Reader and Writer:

```
import java.io.BufferedReader;
import java.io.IOException;
import java.io.InputStreamReader;
import java.io.OutputStreamWriter;
import java.io.PrintWriter;

public class ReaderWriterTester
{
        public static void main(String[] args)
```

```
{
        InputStreamReader inputStreamReader = null;
        BufferedReader bufferedReader = null;
        OutputStreamWriter outputStreamWriter = null;
        PrintWriter printWriter = null;
        try{

                String inputString;

                //wrap System.in
                inputStreamReader = new InputStreamReader(System.in);
                bufferedReader= new BufferedReader(inputStreamReader);

                //wrap System.out
                outputStreamWriter = new OutputStreamWriter(System.out);
                printWriter = new PrintWriter(outputStreamWriter);

                // infinite loop
                while (true)
                {
                    // prompt the user
                    printWriter.print("Enter Something: ");
                    printWriter.flush();

                    // read in a line as string
                    inputString = bufferedReader.readLine();

                    // if the user simply hits the Enter key, exit
                    if (inputString.equals(""))
                    {
                        break;
                    }

                    // print out user input
                    printWriter.println("You have entered: " + inputString);

                }
        }
        catch (IOException e){
            System.out.println(e.toString());
        }
```

```
        finally{
            try{
                //close all the streams
                inputStreamReader.close();
                bufferedReader.close();
                outputStreamWriter.close();
                printWriter.close();
            }
            catch(Exception e){
                //do nothing. probably null pointer exception
            }
        }
    }
}
```

Here is some output:

Enter Something: Hi There

You have entered: Hi There

Enter Something: How are You

You have entered: How are You

File I/O

File I/O is the same as standard I/O, except for two things:

1). We must somehow provide the filename to our I/O class for input or output
2). We can completely avoid 1-byte reading and writing and do 2-bytes character reading and writing directly.

Java has a FileReader class. The constructor of this class takes a string as a filename and opens the file for input.

Java has a FileWriter class. The constructor of this class takes a string as a filename and opens the file for output.

Assuming you have temp folder under your root directory. Copy a text file in \temp folder and rename it to myfile.txt. Run the following program:

```java
import java.io.BufferedReader;
import java.io.FileNotFoundException;
import java.io.FileReader;
import java.io.FileWriter;
import java.io.IOException;
import java.io.PrintWriter;


public class FileIOTester
{
    public static void main(String[] args)
    {
        FileReader fileReader = null;
        BufferedReader bufferedReader = null;
        FileWriter fileWriter = null;
        PrintWriter printWriter = null;
        try{
                String inputString=null;

                fileReader = new FileReader("/temp/myfile.txt");
                bufferedReader= new BufferedReader(fileReader);

                fileWriter = new FileWriter("/temp/myfilecopy.txt");
                printWriter= new PrintWriter(fileWriter);

                // infinite loop
                while (true)
                {
                    // read in a line
                    inputString = bufferedReader.readLine();

                    // if the input is null - end of file, exit the loop
                    if (inputString==null)
                    {
```

```
                          break;
            }
                // write to the file
                printWriter.println(inputString);


            }
            System.out.println("File Copy is complete");
      }
      // catch file not found exception
      catch (FileNotFoundException e)
      {
            System.out.println(e.toString());
      }
      // catch IOException.
      catch (IOException e){
            System.out.println(e.toString());
      }
      finally{
            try{
                fileReader.close();
                bufferedReader.close();
                fileWriter.close();
                printWriter.close();
                }
                catch(Exception e){
                   //nothing to do - probably null pointer exception.
                }
      }
   }
}
```

After running the above program, go back to your \temp folder. You should have a new file called myfilecopy.txt. Open this file. This should be an exact duplicate of myfile.txt.

The File Class

The File class has a deceiving name – you might think it refers to a file, but it does not necessarily do so. It can represent a file or a directory(folder). The file may already exist or about to be created. The second interesting thing about file class is that it tells you everything about a file (and it would even create a new file for you) but it does not let you read from or write to a file. You must provide the File object to the FileReader and FileWriter class for I/O. Fortunately, FileReader and FileWriter accept File object as an argument of their constructors.

Here are some useful methods of File:

Method Name	Return Type	Description
canRead()	boolean	Tests whether the application can read the file denoted by this abstract pathname.
canWrite()	boolean	Tests whether the application can modify to the file denoted by this abstract pathname.
compareTo(File pathname)	Int	Compares two abstract pathnames lexicographically.
createNewFile()	boolean	Atomically creates a new, empty file named by this abstract pathname if and only if a file with this name does not yet exist.
createTempFile(String prefix, String suffix)	static File	Creates an empty file in the default temporary-file directory, using the given prefix and suffix to generate its name.
createTempFile(String prefix, String suffix, File directory)	static File	Creates a new empty file in the specified directory, using the given prefix and suffix strings to generate its name.
delete()	boolean	Deletes the file or directory denoted by this abstract pathname.
deleteOnExit()	Void	Requests that the file or directory denoted by this abstract pathname be deleted when the virtual machine terminates.
equals(Object obj)	boolean	Tests this abstract pathname for equality with the given object.
exists()	boolean	Tests whether the file denoted by this abstract pathname exists.
getName()	String	Returns the name of the file or directory denoted by this abstract pathname.

getParent()	String	Returns the pathname string of this abstract pathname's parent, or null if this pathname does not name a parent directory.
getParentFile()	File	Returns the abstract pathname of this abstract pathname's parent, or null if this pathname does not name a parent directory.
getPath()	String	Converts this abstract pathname into a pathname string.
hashCode()	int	Computes a hash code for this abstract pathname.
isDirectory()	boolean	Tests whether the file denoted by this abstract pathname is a directory.
isFile()	boolean	Tests whether the file denoted by this abstract pathname is a normal file.
isHidden()	boolean	Tests whether the file named by this abstract pathname is a hidden file.
lastModified()	long	Returns the time that the file denoted by this abstract pathname was last modified.
length()	long	Returns the length of the file denoted by this abstract pathname.
list()	String[]	Returns an array of strings naming the files and directories in the directory denoted by this abstract pathname.
list(FilenameFilter filter)	String[]	Returns an array of strings naming the files and directories in the directory denoted by this abstract pathname that satisfy the specified filter.
listFiles()	File[]	Returns an array of abstract pathnames denoting the files in the directory denoted by this abstract pathname.
listFiles(FileFilter filter)	File[]	Returns an array of abstract pathnames denoting the files and directories in the directory denoted by this abstract pathname that satisfy the specified filter.
listFiles(FilenameFilter filter)	File[]	Returns an array of abstract pathnames denoting the files and directories in the directory denoted by this abstract pathname that satisfy the specified filter.

listRoots()	static File[]	List the available filesystem roots like c:\,d:\,e:\
mkdir()	Boolean	Creates the directory named by this abstract pathname.
mkdirs()	Boolean	Creates the directory named by this abstract pathname, including any necessary but nonexistent parent directories.
renameTo(File dest)	Boolean	Renames the file denoted by this abstract pathname.
setLastModified(long time)	Boolean	Sets the last-modified time of the file or directory named by this abstract pathname.
setReadOnly()	Boolean	Marks the file or directory named by this abstract pathname so that only read operations are allowed.
toURL()	URL	Converts this abstract pathname into a file: URL

Here is an example of using the file class:

```java
import java.io.File;
import java.io.IOException;

public class FileObjectTester{
    public static void main(String[] args){
        try{
            File file = new File ("/temp/myfile.txt");

            if (!file.exists()){
                System.out.println("File does not exist, creating new
file");
                file.createNewFile();
                return;
            }
            if (file.isFile()){
                System.out.println("Found your file");

                // get the file size.
                System.out.println("File size: " + file.length());
```

```
                    System.out.println();


            }


            // if directory show the directory listing
            if (file.isDirectory()){
                System.out.println("Found your folder");
                System.out.println("Files in the folder: ");


                // get the file names in the directory
                String[] strFiles = file.list();


                // loop through the files and display them
                for (int nI=0; nI < strFiles.length;nI++){
                    System.out.println("   " +strFiles[nI]);
                }
                System.out.println();
            }
            // show attributes
            System.out.println("Readable: " + file.canRead());
            System.out.println("Writable: " + file.canWrite());
            System.out.println("Hidden: " + file.isHidden());
            System.out.println("Absolute path: " + file.getAbsolutePath());
            System.out.println("Name: " + file.getName());
            System.out.println();


            File[] drives;


            // get the drive letters on the machine.
            drives=File.listRoots();
            System.out.println("Here are the Drives: ");


            // loop through the drive names and print them
            for (int nI=0; nI < drives.length;nI++){
                System.out.println("       " +drives[nI].toString());
            }
    }
    // catch IOException.
    catch (IOException e){
            System.out.println(e.toString());
```

```
        }
    }
}
```

Assuming you have myfile.txt in \temp folder, run the code and you will see all the information about your file.

If you have a \temp folder but no myfile.txt, run the code and it will create a new empty file called myfile.txt

Change the following line of code:

```
File file = new File ("/temp/myfile.txt");
```

To:

```
File file = new File ("/temp");
```

Assuming you have a /temp folder, it will print all the filenames in the folder. Cool, right?

Section B

Multithreading and Network Programming

Chapter 11

What is an Operating System?

Operating System is the most important program that runs on a computer. Every computer must have an operating system to run other programs. Operating systems perform basic tasks, such as recognizing input from the keyboard and mouse, sending output to the screen, keeping track of files and directories on the disk, and controlling peripheral devices such as disk drives and printers.

What is Multitasking?

Let's first discuss what a process or task is. A process is a computer program in execution. In the good old days, you could only run one process at a time on a computer. Things evolved and suddenly you can run many processes simultaneously and hence the term Multitasking was introduced.

What is Multithreading?

Soon, it became obvious that even Multitasking is not good enough. We should be able to break up each process into smaller pieces and be able to execute them simultaneously. These sub-processes are called "Execution Threads" or simply "Threads". Multithreading is the ability of an operating system to execute threads simultaneously. The programmer must carefully design the program in such a way that all the threads can run at the same time without interfering with each other.

While the whole JVM is merely one process in your operating system, Java allows you to turn your application into separate, independently-running subtasks or threads. Simply put, in Java, you can create your own threads.

Before we go any further with threads, it is important that we understand how multitasking works. A process is a running program with its own address space. A multitasking operating system gives us the illusion that more than one process is running at a time by periodically providing CPU cycles to each process. So, these processes are taking theirs turns to use the CPU, but these swapping are happening so quickly that it looks like all the processes are running all the time.

A single process can, in turn, be broken down into multiple concurrently executing threads. That's why a thread is also called a lightweight process. It functions very much like a process but the overhead of running a thread is much less compared to a process. The CPU time that a process gets is further divided into smaller pieces and given to each thread. So, the threads are taking their turns within a process giving us the illusion that the threads are also running simultaneously. The following picture might give you a visual:

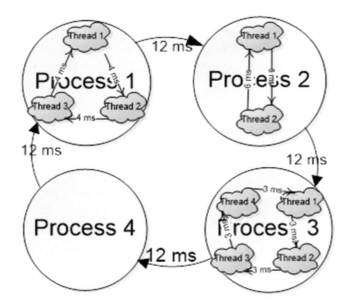

Thread Class

You can start with your Thread programming by sub-classing the Thread class that comes with Java API. The sub-class must override the run() method since the code inside the run() method would run on a separate thread. Once your thread class is written, you create an object from your thread class. After the thread object is created, you can configure it. Configuring a thread involves setting its initial priority, name and so on. When the thread is ready to run, you invoke its start() method (not its run() method). The start method spawns a new thread of execution. The start method throws an IllegalThreadStateException if the thread you are trying to start has already been started. The virtual machine then invokes the new thread's run method, making the thread active. When the run method of a thread returns the thread has exited.

Here are some useful methods of Thread class:

start()	void	Causes this thread to begin execution; the Java Virtual Machine calls the run method of this thread after this method.
run()	void	If this thread was constructed by sub-classing Thread then the code in this method runs on a separate thread.
setName(String name)	void	Changes the name of this thread to be equal to the argument name.
getName()	String	Returns this thread's name.
setPriority(int new-Priority)	void	Changes the priority of this thread.
getPriority()	int	Returns this thread's priority.
sleep(long millis)	static void	Causes the currently executing thread to sleep (temporarily cease execution) for the specified number of milliseconds.

`sleep(long millis, int nanos)`	static void	Causes the currently executing thread to sleep (cease execution) for the specified number of milliseconds plus the specified number of nanoseconds.
`yield()`	static void	Causes the currently executing thread object to temporarily pause and allow other threads to execute.
`interrupt()`	void	Interrupts this thread.
`isInterrupted()`	boolean	Tests whether this thread has been interrupted.
`interrupted()`	static boolean	Tests whether the current thread has been interrupted.
`isAlive()`	boolean	Tests if this thread is alive.
`setDaemon(boolean on)`	void	Marks this thread as either a daemon thread or a user thread.
`isDaemon()`	boolean	Tests if this thread is a daemon thread.
`dumpStack()`	static void	Prints a stack trace of the current thread.
`join()`	void	Waits for this thread to die.
`join(long millis)`	void	Waits at most milliseconds for this thread to die.
`join(long millis, int nanos)`	void	Waits at most milliseconds plus nanos nanoseconds for this thread to die.
`toString()`	String	Returns a string representation of this thread, including the thread's name, priority, and thread group.

Here is an example of sub-classing Thread. This thread will generate random number, sleep for a while and then generate another random number:

```
public class RandomThread extends Thread{
    public void run(){
```

```
        System.out.println("RandomThread Running");
        // temp variable to store random number
        int randomNumber;
        try
        {
                for (int i=0;i<10;i++){
                        // generate a random number between 20 and 30
                        randomNumber=(int) ((30 - 20 + 1) * Math.random() + 20);
                        // print it
                        System.out.print(randomNumber);

                        // put the current thread to sleep for 500 msec = 1/2 sec
                        Thread.sleep(500);
                        // print a tab
                        System.out.print("\t");
                }
        }
        //sleep method throws this exception
        catch(InterruptedException e)
        {
                e.printStackTrace();
        }
        System.out.println();
        System.out.println("RandomThread Finished");
    }
}
```

Here is the tester:

```
public class RandomThreadTester {
    public static void main(String[] args){
        System.out.println("main Method Started");
        RandomThread randomThread= new RandomThread();
        randomThread.start();
        System.out.println("main Method Finished");
    }
}
```

Here is the output:

```
main Method Started
```

```
main Method Finished
RandomThread Running
28    23    29    30    22    24    20    20    22    29
RandomThread Finished
```

As you can see from the above output, the main method started and finished before the thread even starts running.. How is that possible? There must be two threads involved here then, right? Yes, there is, which is our next topic.

The Main Thread

In every Java application, even without any thread programming, there is at least one thread, the "main" thread. The purpose of the main thread is to execute the main() method. If your application creates no other threads, the application will finish the main thread when main() method returns and that will be end of the applications run. But if we create other threads, what happens to the other threads when the main() method returns? Well, the simple answer is the other threads continue to run and application will not end until all the other threads are done. That's exactly what we saw above (there is one exception to this – daemon thread, we will discuss that later).

We can slightly change the RandomThread and RandomThreadTester to show the thread names as follows:

```java
public class RandomThread extends Thread{
    public void run()
    {
        System.out.println("Starting Thread: " +
Thread.currentThread().getName());
        // temp variable to store random number
        int randomNumber;
        try
        {
            for (int i=0;i<10;i++){
                // generate a random number between 20 and 30
                randomNumber=(int) ((30 - 20 + 1) * Math.random() + 20);
                // print it
                System.out.print(randomNumber);
```

```
                // put the current thread to sleep for 500 msec = 1/2 sec
                Thread.sleep(500);
                // print a tab
                System.out.print("\t");
            }
        }
        //sleep method throws this exception
        catch(InterruptedException e)
        {
                e.printStackTrace();
        }
        System.out.println();
        System.out.println("Ending Thread: " +
Thread.currentThread().getName());
    }
}


public class RandomThreadTester {
    public static void main(String[] args){
        System.out.println("Starting Thread: " +
Thread.currentThread().getName());
        RandomThread randomThread= new RandomThread();
        randomThread.start();
        System.out.println("Ending Thread: " +
Thread.currentThread().getName());
    }
}
```

Here is the output:

```
Starting Thread: main
Ending Thread: main
Starting Thread: Thread-0
24     28     25     20     25     20     22     28     20     29
Ending Thread: Thread-0
```

Notice how the main thread is named "main" but our RandomThread is named "Thread-0". We can fix this by giving our thread a friendly name by calling its setName() method.

Runnable Interface

Sub-classing thread may be fine in many instances but there is another way to create your own thread and often this is a preferred way. In this process you need to follow a few steps:

1). You implement an interface called Runnable in a class that you write. The Runnable interface has only one abstract run() method that you need to implement.
2). You then create an object from this class.
3). You then create an object from plain Thread class and pass your runnable object to the constructor of the Thread class.
4). Finally, you call the start() method on the Thread object.

The JVM will end up calling the run method that you just wrote in a new thread of execution. The steps above sound complicate. It is a lot easier to understand by looking at an example. Let's write the random number generation thread using this approach as follows:

```java
public class RandomRunnable implements Runnable {
    public void run()
    {
        System.out.println("Starting Thread: " +
Thread.currentThread().getName());

        // temp variable to store random number
        int randomNumber;
        try
        {
            for (int i=0;i<10;i++){
                // generate a random number between 20 and 30
                randomNumber=(int) ((30 - 20 + 1) * Math.random() + 20);
                // print it
                System.out.print(randomNumber);

                // put the current thread to sleep for 500 msec = 1/2 sec
                Thread.sleep(500);
                // print a tab
                System.out.print("\t");
            }
```

```
    }
    //sleep method throws this exception
    catch(InterruptedException e)
    {
            e.printStackTrace();
    }
    System.out.println();
    System.out.println("Ending Thread: " +
Thread.currentThread().getName());
    }
}
```

That was just step 1 of the process. Rest of the steps go the tester as follows:

```
public class RandomRunnableTester {
    public static void main(String[] args) {
            System.out.println("Starting Thread: " +
Thread.currentThread().getName());
            RandomRunnable myRunnable = new RandomRunnable(); //step 2
            Thread thread = new Thread(myRunnable); // step 3
            thread.start(); // step 4
            System.out.println("Ending Thread: " +
Thread.currentThread().getName());
    }
}
```

The output would be the same as before.

Benefits of using Runnable Interface

So, you can accomplish the same task by sub-classing Thread or by implementing Runnable interface, but it seems the Runnable interface requires more work. So why is this any better? Here is why. When you implement Runnable interface you still can sub-class another class at the same time. When you simply sub-class Thread you don't have that luxury because Java only support single inheritance. For that reason, Runnable interface is often preferred.

Thread States

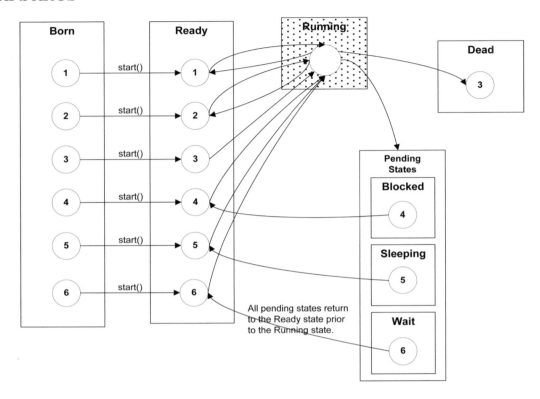

At any time, a thread is said to be in one of the several states. When a thread object is created, it is in the "born" state. The thread remains in this state until the thread's start() method is invoked. The call to the start() method causes the thread to enter the "ready" state (also known as the Runnable State). The highest priority ready thread enters the running state when the system assigns a processor to the thread. A thread enters the "dead" state when its run method completes or terminates for any reason.

A running thread can enter the "blocked" state when the thread issues an input/output request. In this case, the blocked thread becomes ready when the I/O it is waiting for completes.

When a sleep() method is called on a running thread, that thread enters the "sleeping" state. A sleeping thread becomes ready after the designated sleep time expires.

When a running thread calls wait() method on an object, the thread enters a "waiting" state for the particular object on which wait was called. A waiting thread becomes ready when another thread calls notify() or notifyAll() on the same object that cause the wait.

A thread can call the yield() method to give another thread a chance to execute.

Thread Priority

Every thread has a priority in the range of 1 and 10. By default, each thread is given priority 5. These three priorities of thread are defined by the following constants in Thread class:

```
public final static int MAX  PRIORITY//    10
public final static int MIN  PRIORITY//    1
public final static int NORM  PRIORITY     //5    default priority of a thread.
```

However, you can assign any priority between 1 and 10 to a thread. A thread's priority can be adjusted by calling a method setPriority(). The method getPriority() returns the thread's priority.

Concurrency Problem with Threads

Our BankAccount class and all its sub-classes work fine if one thread operates on one object. However, if two or more threads operate on the same account, there is a possibility of interleaved operations that can corrupt the data. Imagine, one thread that is executing the deposit method while the other is executing the withdrawal method – the balance field could easily get corrupted if this happens.

Since the real interleaving is unpredictable and therefore, hard to reproduce on simple methods like deposit() and withdrawal(), we have to open up the door for interleaving by breaking the operation into small pieces (this would happen in machine registry level anyway) and by introducing random sleep into these two methods.

To keep our focus on this concurrency issue we will use a non-abstract and simpler version of BankAccount with only balance field and modify it.

Here is our BankAccount class with balance only and with some additional execution trace statements and sleeps:

```java
public class BankAccount{
        private double balance;

        public void deposit(double amount, int n){
                try{
                        System.out.println("Deposit #" + n +" started by " + Thread.currentThread().getName());

                        /* break the deposit in 3 steps
                         * like it will happen at hardware level
                         * and introduce sleep before the final
                         * modification of balance to simulate
                         * concurrency issue
                         */
                        double temp1 = balance; //step 1 - read the balance
                        temp1 = temp1 + amount; // step 2 - increment balance in a temp variable
                        int random = (int) (Math.random()*100);
                        System.out.println("Deposit #" + n + " sleeping for: " + random +" ms by " + Thread.currentThread().getName());
                        Thread.sleep(random);
                        balance = temp1; // step 3 - update the balance
                        System.out.println("after deposit #" + n + " the balance is " + balance);
                        random = (int) (Math.random()*100);
                        System.out.println("Deposit #" + n + " sleeping again for: " + random +" ms by " + Thread.currentThread().getName());
                        Thread.sleep(random);
                        System.out.println("Deposit #" + n +" finished by " + Thread.currentThread().getName());
                }
                catch(InterruptedException e){
                        e.printStackTrace();
                }
        }

        public void withdrawal(double amount, int n){
```

```
        try{
                System.out.println("Withdrawal #" + n +" started by " + Thread.
currentThread().getName());


                /* break the withdrawal in 3 steps
                 * like it will happen at hardware level
                 * and introduce sleep before the final
                 * modification of balance to simulate
                 * concurrency issue
                 */
                double temp1 = balance; //step 1 - read the balance
                temp1 = temp1 - amount; // step 2 - decrement balance in a temp
variable
                int random = (int) (Math.random()*100);
                System.out.println("Withdrawal #" + n + " sleeping for: " +
random +" ms by " + Thread.currentThread().getName());
                Thread.sleep(random);
                balance = temp1; // step 3 - update the balance
                System.out.println("after withdrawal #" + n + " the balance is "
+ balance);

                random = (int) (Math.random()*100);
                System.out.println("Withdrawal #" + n + " sleeping again for: " +
random +" ms by " + Thread.currentThread().getName());
                Thread.sleep(random);
                System.out.println("Withdrawal #" + n +" finished by " + Thread.
currentThread().getName());
            }
            catch(InterruptedException e){
                e.printStackTrace();
            }
        }


    public double getBalance(){
            return balance;
        }
}
```

Now that we have broken down deposit() and withdrawal() into hardware steps and added sleeps that simulates CPU switching between threads, let's write the following 2 Threads, one will do 4 deposits and the other one will do 4 withdrawals:

```java
public class DepositThread extends Thread{
       private BankAccount bankAccount;

       DepositThread(BankAccount anyBankAccount){
              super();
              bankAccount=anyBankAccount;
       }

       public void run(){
              // loops 4 times
              for (int n=1; n<=4; n++)
              {
                     // calls deposit of bankaccount with deposit number n.
                     bankAccount.deposit(600,n);
              }
       }
}


public class WithdrawalThread extends Thread{
       private BankAccount bankAccount;

       WithdrawalThread(BankAccount anyBankAccount){
              super();
              bankAccount=anyBankAccount;
       }

       public void run(){
              // loops 4 times
              for (int n=1; n<=4; n++)
              {
                     // calls deposit of bankaccount with deposit number n.
                     bankAccount.withdrawal(600,n);
              }
       }
}
```

To reproduce concurrency issues, these two threads must share one and only one BankAccount object.

Here is the driver that will kick off these threads with one and only one BankAccount object:

```java
public class ConcurrencyDriver {
    public static void main(String[] args) {
        try {
            BankAccount b = new BankAccount();
            DepositThread dt = new DepositThread(b);
            dt.setName("Deposit Thread");
            WithdrawalThread wt = new WithdrawalThread(b);
            wt.setName("Withdrawal Thread");
            dt.start();
            wt.start();
            Thread.sleep(1000); // 1 second sleep
            System.out.println("Final balance reported by: " + Thread.
currentThread().getName() + " " + b.getBalance()); }
        catch (InterruptedException e) {
            e.printStackTrace();
        }
    }
}
```

Notice I have introduced a delay in main() before checking the balance so that the two threads get enough time to finish before we check balance.

In theory after 4 deposits of $600 and 4 withdrawal of $600 your balance should be back to zero – they should cancel each other out. After running the driver, you will see that the balance rarely become zero. Run it several times, the final balance will vary each time.

Here is one output:

```
Withdrawal #1 started by Withdrawal Thread
Deposit #1 started by Deposit Thread
Withdrawal #1 sleeping for: 7 ms by Withdrawal Thread
Deposit #1 sleeping for: 56 ms by Deposit Thread
```

```
after withdrawal #1 the balance is -600.0
Withdrawal #1 sleeping again for: 80 ms by Withdrawal Thread
after deposit #1 the balance is 600.0
Deposit #1 sleeping again for: 62 ms by Deposit Thread
Withdrawal #1 finished by Withdrawal Thread
Withdrawal #2 started by Withdrawal Thread
Withdrawal #2 sleeping for: 63 ms by Withdrawal Thread
Deposit #1 finished by Deposit Thread
Deposit #2 started by Deposit Thread
Deposit #2 sleeping for: 95 ms by Deposit Thread
after withdrawal #2 the balance is 0.0
Withdrawal #2 sleeping again for: 96 ms by Withdrawal Thread
after deposit #2 the balance is 1200.0
Deposit #2 sleeping again for: 84 ms by Deposit Thread
Withdrawal #2 finished by Withdrawal Thread
Withdrawal #3 started by Withdrawal Thread
Withdrawal #3 sleeping for: 89 ms by Withdrawal Thread
Deposit #2 finished by Deposit Thread
Deposit #3 started by Deposit Thread
Deposit #3 sleeping for: 62 ms by Deposit Thread
after withdrawal #3 the balance is 600.0
Withdrawal #3 sleeping again for: 42 ms by Withdrawal Thread
after deposit #3 the balance is 1800.0
Deposit #3 sleeping again for: 17 ms by Deposit Thread
Deposit #3 finished by Deposit Thread
Deposit #4 started by Deposit Thread
Deposit #4 sleeping for: 40 ms by Deposit Thread
Withdrawal #3 finished by Withdrawal Thread
Withdrawal #4 started by Withdrawal Thread
Withdrawal #4 sleeping for: 47 ms by Withdrawal Thread
after deposit #4 the balance is 2400.0
```

```
Deposit #4 sleeping again for: 7 ms by Deposit Thread

after withdrawal #4 the balance is 1200.0

Withdrawal #4 sleeping again for: 72 ms by Withdrawal Thread

Deposit #4 finished by Deposit Thread

Withdrawal #4 finished by Withdrawal Thread

Final balance reported by: main 1200.0
```

Notice how deposit and withdrawals are interleaving causing concurrency problem.

Synchronized Methods

To make a class usable in a multithreaded environment, appropriate methods are usually declared synchronized by using the keyword "synchronized" in their declaration. What are the appropriate methods? Here is the rule. For each field that can cause concurrency issues, all the getters and setters of the field must be synchronized. Ok, the setters make sense, why the getters? Well, reading data from a field may also happen in multiple steps and incomplete read is possible. Hence, similar safeguard is needed for getters too. Also, if a field is int or smaller, no need to synchronize, int or smaller fields are atomic at the hardware level, operations on them happens in one step.

Our BankAccount's balance is a double, bigger than int and requires synchronization. There are 2 setters – deposit() and withdrawal() and 1 getter getBalance() for the balance field. All three should be synchronized.

One more thing. Synchronization is not physical lock, it is merely a flag and only synchronized methods honor the flag. If one thread invokes a synchronized method on an object, that object is flagged as dirty, another thread invoking a synchronized method on that same object will block until the flag is released. However, an unsynchronized method would be happy to operate on the object regardless of the state of the flag. Hence, care must be taken to synchronize ALL the methods related to a field. However, constructors do not need to be synchronized even if they are setters since they are executed only during object creation and that can happen in only one thread for any given new object. In other words, it is not possible that two threads are running the constructors of one object.

Here is our BankAccount with synchronized methods:

```java
public class BankAccount{
        private double balance;


        public synchronized void deposit(double amount, int n){
                try{

                        System.out.println("Deposit #" + n +" started by " + Thread.
currentThread().getName());

                                /* break the deposit in 3 steps
                                * like it will happen at hardware level
                                * and introduce sleep before the final
                                * modification of balance to simulate
                                * concurrency issue
                                */
                                double temp1 = balance; //step 1 - read the balance
                                temp1 = temp1 + amount; // step 2 - increment balance in a temp
variable
                                int random = (int) (Math.random()*100);
                                System.out.println("Deposit #" + n + " sleeping for: " + random
+" ms by " + Thread.currentThread().getName());
                                Thread.sleep(random);
                                balance = temp1; // step 3 - update the balance
                                System.out.println("after deposit #" + n + " the balance is " +
balance);

                                random = (int) (Math.random()*100);
                                System.out.println("Deposit #" + n + " sleeping again for: " +
random +" ms by " + Thread.currentThread().getName());
                                Thread.sleep(random);
                                System.out.println("Deposit #" + n +" finished by " + Thread.
currentThread().getName());
                        }
                        catch(InterruptedException e){
                                e.printStackTrace();
                        }
        }


        public synchronized void withdrawal(double amount, int n){
```

```
            try{
                    System.out.println("Withdrawal #" + n +" started by " + Thread.
currentThread().getName());


                    /* break the withdrawal in 3 steps
                     * like it will happen at hardware level
                     * and introduce sleep before the final
                     * modification of balance to simulate
                     * concurrency issue
                     */
                    double temp1 = balance; //step 1 - read the balance
                    temp1 = temp1 - amount; // step 2 - decrement balance in a temp
variable
                    int random = (int) (Math.random()*100);
                    System.out.println("Withdrawal #" + n + " sleeping for: " +
random +" ms by " + Thread.currentThread().getName());
                    Thread.sleep(random);
                    balance = temp1; // step 3 - update the balance
                    System.out.println("after withdrawal #" + n + " the balance is "
+ balance);

                    random = (int) (Math.random()*100);
                    System.out.println("Withdrawal #" + n + " sleeping again for: " +
random +" ms by " + Thread.currentThread().getName());
                    Thread.sleep(random);
                    System.out.println("Withdrawal #" + n +" finished by " + Thread.
currentThread().getName());
            }
            catch(InterruptedException e){
                    e.printStackTrace();
            }
        }


        public synchronized double getBalance(){
                return balance;
        }
    }
}
```

Now all the getters and setter for balance is synchronized. If we run the driver again, here is the output:

```
Withdrawal #1 started by Withdrawal Thread
```

```
Withdrawal #1 sleeping for: 0 ms by Withdrawal Thread
after withdrawal #1 the balance is -600.0
Withdrawal #1 sleeping again for: 21 ms by Withdrawal Thread
Withdrawal #1 finished by Withdrawal Thread
Withdrawal #2 started by Withdrawal Thread
Withdrawal #2 sleeping for: 50 ms by Withdrawal Thread
after withdrawal #2 the balance is -1200.0
Withdrawal #2 sleeping again for: 88 ms by Withdrawal Thread
Withdrawal #2 finished by Withdrawal Thread
Withdrawal #3 started by Withdrawal Thread
Withdrawal #3 sleeping for: 56 ms by Withdrawal Thread
after withdrawal #3 the balance is -1800.0
Withdrawal #3 sleeping again for: 55 ms by Withdrawal Thread
Withdrawal #3 finished by Withdrawal Thread
Deposit #1 started by Deposit Thread
Deposit #1 sleeping for: 20 ms by Deposit Thread
after deposit #1 the balance is -1200.0
Deposit #1 sleeping again for: 44 ms by Deposit Thread
Deposit #1 finished by Deposit Thread
Deposit #2 started by Deposit Thread
Deposit #2 sleeping for: 10 ms by Deposit Thread
after deposit #2 the balance is -600.0
Deposit #2 sleeping again for: 72 ms by Deposit Thread
Deposit #2 finished by Deposit Thread
Deposit #3 started by Deposit Thread
Deposit #3 sleeping for: 42 ms by Deposit Thread

after deposit #3 the balance is 0.0
Deposit #3 sleeping again for: 15 ms by Deposit Thread
Deposit #3 finished by Deposit Thread
Withdrawal #4 started by Withdrawal Thread
```

```
Withdrawal #4 sleeping for: 77 ms by Withdrawal Thread
after withdrawal #4 the balance is -600.0
Withdrawal #4 sleeping again for: 90 ms by Withdrawal Thread
Withdrawal #4 finished by Withdrawal Thread
Deposit #4 started by Deposit Thread
Deposit #4 sleeping for: 37 ms by Deposit Thread
after deposit #4 the balance is 0.0
Deposit #4 sleeping again for: 22 ms by Deposit Thread
Deposit #4 finished by Deposit Thread
Final balance reported by: main 0.0
```

No matter how many times you run the driver, you will see two things consistently:

a). Although we can't tell whether a deposit or a withdrawal would start first, a deposit or withdrawal that starts always finishes before any other method executes.

b). At the end, the balance would always be zero.

Synchronizing Static Methods

Static methods can also be synchronized. Static synchronization locks the class instead of the object. Two threads cannot execute synchronized static methods on the same class at the same time. The per-class lock for a static method has no effect on any regular non-static methods of that class. When a class is locked only other synchronized static methods are blocked. Similarly, per-object locks have no effect on any static methods.

Synchronization and Inheritance

When an extended class overrides a synchronized method, the new method can be synchronized or unsynchronized. The superclass's method will still be synchronized. If the unsynchronized method calls the superclass's synchronized method, the object will be locked at that time and will be unlocked as soon as the superclass's method returns. Similarly, when an extended class overrides an unsynchronized method, the new method can be synchronized or unsynchronized.

Synchronized Block

Synchronizing a method has four shortcomings:

1). It does not come without performance penalty. Most of the time, in a method, you don't need to lock the whole method, only a fraction of the method code that manipulates shared fields needs to be locked. Such segment of a method is known as "Critical Section".

2). Synchronized method always locks the object on which the method is located. Sometimes you need to lock some other object than the current object, but you can't.

3). If you receive a third-party Java code where methods are not synchronized but you want to make sure the third-party object is locked - you cannot do that.

4). Sometimes you have the opposite problem of a). You want to expand the scope of the lock beyond one method. For example, you want to do deposit() followed by getBalance() before the lock is released because, even if they are individually synchronized, object will be unlocked between the two method calls and there is a slight possibility that the object may be modified by another thread between your deposit() and getBalance() call. The probability of such incident is extremely low but certainly not zero.

Java solves all the above four issues by introducing synchronized block. The synchronized block enables you to lock an object while executing a small block of code. The general form of synchronized statement is as follows:

```
synchronized (Object reference)
{
        // some code

}
```

Now, with the introduction of synchronized block,

a). you can mark only the "Critical Section" of a method as synchronized block, resulting huge performance enhancement as follows:

```
synchronized (this)
{
```

```
                // some code in critical section
        }
```

We will see details of this approach shortly.

b). You can lock some other object in your code as follows:

```
public class SynchronizedBlockOtherObject extends Thread {
        private int[] myArray;

        public SynchronizedBlockOtherObject(int[] anyArray){ //Constructor
            myArray=anyArray;
        }
        public void run(){

            synchronized(myArray){ //lock the array
                    myArray[0]=10; //now change value
            }
        }
}
```

Let's rewrite the BankAccount with synchronized block as follows:

```
public class BankAccount{
        private double balance;

        public void deposit(double amount, int n){
            try{
                    System.out.println("Deposit #" + n +" started by " +
Thread.currentThread().getName());

                            /* break the deposit in 3 steps
                             * like it will happen at hardware level
                             * and introduce sleep before the final
                             * modification of balance to simulate
                             * concurrency issue
                             */
                            int random=0;
                            synchronized(this){ //critical section, lock the object
```

```
                            double temp1 = balance; //step 1 - read the balance
                            temp1 = temp1 + amount; // step 2 - increment balance
in a temp variable
                            random = (int) (Math.random()*100);
                            System.out.println("Deposit #" + n + " sleeping for: " +
random +" ms by " + Thread.currentThread().getName());
                            Thread.sleep(random);
                            balance = temp1; // step 3 - update the balance
                            System.out.println("after deposit #" + n + " the balance
is " + balance);

                            } //end of critical section
                            random = (int) (Math.random()*100);
                            System.out.println("Deposit #" + n + " sleeping again
for: " + random +" ms by " + Thread.currentThread().getName());
                            Thread.sleep(random);
                            System.out.println("Deposit #" + n +" finished by " +
Thread.currentThread().getName());
                  }
            catch(InterruptedException e){
                        e.printStackTrace();
            }
      }

      public void withdrawal(double amount, int n){
            try{

                  System.out.println("Withdrawal #" + n +" started by " + Thread.
currentThread().getName());

                  /* break the withdrawal in 3 steps
                   * like it will happen at hardware level
                   * and introduce sleep before the final
                   * modification of balance to simulate
                   * concurrency issue
                   */
                  int random=0;
                  synchronized(this){ //critical section, lock the object
                     double temp1 = balance; //step 1 - read the balance
                     temp1 = temp1 - amount; // step 2 - decrement balance in a
temp variable
                     random = (int) (Math.random()*100);
                     System.out.println("Withdrawal #" + n + " sleeping for: " +
```

```
random +" ms by " + Thread.currentThread().getName());
                    Thread.sleep(random);
                    balance = temp1; // step 3 - update the balance
                    System.out.println("after withdrawal #" + n + " the balance is
" + balance);
                } //end of critical section
                random = (int)  (Math.random()*100);
                System.out.println("Withdrawal #" + n + " sleeping again for: " +
random +" ms by " + Thread.currentThread().getName());
                Thread.sleep(random);
                System.out.println("Withdrawal #" + n +" finished by " + Thread.
currentThread().getName());
        }
        catch(InterruptedException e){
                e.printStackTrace();
        }
    }


    public synchronized double getBalance(){
        return balance;
    }
}
```

Notice we used synchronized block in deposit() and withdrawal() but let the getBalance() method as synchronized method. That's because getBalance() method has only one line, we can do synchronized block in getBalance() too, but synchronized block will not improve its performance anyway.

If we run the driver now, you will get output like this:

```
Withdrawal #1 started by Withdrawal Thread
Deposit #1 started by Deposit Thread
Withdrawal #1 sleeping for: 72 ms by Withdrawal Thread
after withdrawal #1 the balance is -600.0
Withdrawal #1 sleeping again for: 6 ms by Withdrawal Thread
Deposit #1 sleeping for: 8 ms by Deposit Thread
Withdrawal #1 finished by Withdrawal Thread
```

```
Withdrawal #2 started by Withdrawal Thread
after deposit #1 the balance is 0.0
Deposit #1 sleeping again for: 51 ms by Deposit Thread
Withdrawal #2 sleeping for: 31 ms by Withdrawal Thread
after withdrawal #2 the balance is -600.0
Withdrawal #2 sleeping again for: 33 ms by Withdrawal Thread
Deposit #1 finished by Deposit Thread
Deposit #2 started by Deposit Thread
Deposit #2 sleeping for: 72 ms by Deposit Thread
Withdrawal #2 finished by Withdrawal Thread
Withdrawal #3 started by Withdrawal Thread
after deposit #2 the balance is 0.0
Deposit #2 sleeping again for: 47 ms by Deposit Thread
Withdrawal #3 sleeping for: 99 ms by Withdrawal Thread
Deposit #2 finished by Deposit Thread
Deposit #3 started by Deposit Thread
after withdrawal #3 the balance is -600.0
Deposit #3 sleeping for: 60 ms by Deposit Thread
Withdrawal #3 sleeping again for: 87 ms by Withdrawal Thread
after deposit #3 the balance is 0.0
Deposit #3 sleeping again for: 11 ms by Deposit Thread
Deposit #3 finished by Deposit Thread
Deposit #4 started by Deposit Thread
Deposit #4 sleeping for: 39 ms by Deposit Thread
Withdrawal #3 finished by Withdrawal Thread
Withdrawal #4 started by Withdrawal Thread
after deposit #4 the balance is 600.0
Deposit #4 sleeping again for: 57 ms by Deposit Thread
Withdrawal #4 sleeping for: 24 ms by Withdrawal Thread
after withdrawal #4 the balance is 0.0
Withdrawal #4 sleeping again for: 85 ms by Withdrawal Thread
```

```
Deposit #4 finished by Deposit Thread
Withdrawal #4 finished by Withdrawal Thread
Final balance reported by: main 0.0
```

Notice, deposit() and withdrawal() are interleaved again!!! However, since the critical section of these methods are protected, there is no way the balance is going to be incorrect. The final balance will turn up to be zero every single time.

Wait(), notify() and notifyAll()

The synchronized locking mechanism keeps threads from interfering with one another, but it lacks the ability to temporary unlock the object and communicate such event with other threads. The following methods, defined in Object class (not in Thread class), allow threads to unlock and communicate with one another:

Thread related methods inherited from Object class		
wait()	void	When called within synchronized area, causes current thread to unlock the object (which has been locked) and wait until another thread invokes the notify() method or the notifyAll() method for the object.
wait(long timeout)	void	When called within synchronized area, causes current thread to unlock the object and wait until either the specified amount of time has elapsed or another thread invokes the notify() method or the notifyAll() method for the object.
wait(long timeout, int nanos)	void	When called within synchronized area, causes current thread to unlock the object and wait until either the specified amount of time has elapsed or another thread invokes the notify() method or the notifyAll() method for the object, or some other thread interrupts the current thread.
notify()	void	Wakes up a single thread that is waiting on this object's lock. If several threads are waiting, you have no control over which thread is notified, in which case it is better to use notifyAll(). If no threads are waiting, the method does nothing.

notifyAll()	void	Wakes up all threads that are waiting on this object's lock.

Although wait(), notify() and notifyAll() methods are derived from the Object class you can't always call them. Here is the rule:

"You should only call these methods from and within a synchronized method or from and within a synchronized block otherwise an IlegalMonitorStateException is thrown at runtime".

One of the very import aspects of the definition of wait() is that when it pauses the thread, it automatically releases the lock on the object. When the waiting thread is restarted the lock is automatically regained again.

To see the usage of wait() and notifyAll() methods let's imagine the following problem: There is an ArrayList of integer shared by two threads 1) ProducerThread and 2) ConsumerThread. The ProducerThread puts 3 random integers in the ArrayList only if the ArrayList is empty, otherwise waits for it to become empty. The ConsumerThread consumes all 3 integers only if there are items on the ArrayList, otherwise it waits to be filled. It other words they take turn. This will go on twice then both threads exit. There is only one problem. To check the emptiness of the ArrayList both Threads must lock the ArrayList but if the condition is not right, they also must unlock the ArrayList immediately. How do they do that? Using synchronized and wait() notifyAll() .

Here is the Producer:

```java
import java.util.ArrayList;


public class ProducerThread extends Thread {
    private ArrayList<Integer> list;
    public ProducerThread(ArrayList<Integer> anyList){
        list=anyList;
    }
    public void run(){
        System.out.println(Thread.currentThread().getName() + " starting");
        for(int i=0;i<2;i++){ // produces twice before exits
            try {
                synchronized(list){
                    while(list.size()!=0){ //list is NOT empty yet, so
wait
```

```
System.out.println(Thread.currentThread().getName() + " going to wait");
                            list.wait();
                }
                for (int j=0;j<3;j++){ // 3 random number
                        int r = (int) (Math.random()*100);
System.out.println(Thread.currentThread().getName() + " produced: " + r);
                        list.add(r);
                }
                list.notifyAll(); //list is full, time to notify
            }
        } catch (InterruptedException e) {
            e.printStackTrace();
        }
    }
    System.out.println(Thread.currentThread().getName() + " ending");
  }
}
```

Here is the Consumer:
```
import java.util.ArrayList;


public class ConsumerThread extends Thread {
      private ArrayList<Integer> list;
      public ConsumerThread(ArrayList<Integer> anyList){
          list=anyList;
      }
      public void run(){
          System.out.println(Thread.currentThread().getName() + " starting");
          for(int i=0;i<2;i++){ // produces twice before exits
              try {
                  synchronized(list){
                      while(list.size()==0){ //list is empty so wait
System.out.println(Thread.currentThread().getName() + " going to wait");
                          list.wait();
                      }
                      for (int j=0;j<3;j++){ // consume 3 random number
                          int c = list.remove(0);
System.out.println(Thread.currentThread().getName() + " consumed: " + c);
```

```
                                }
                                list.notifyAll(); // list is empty again, time to
notify
                        }
                } catch (InterruptedException e) {
                    e.printStackTrace();
                }
            }
            System.out.println(Thread.currentThread().getName() + " ending");
        }
    }
}
```

Here is the driver:

```
import java.util.ArrayList;


public class ProducerConsumerDriver {
    public static void main(String[] args) {
        ArrayList<Integer> myList = new ArrayList<Ingeter>();
        ProducerThread pt = new ProducerThread(myList);
        pt.setName("Producer Thread");
        ConsumerThread ct = new ConsumerThread(myList);
        ct.setName("Consumer Thread");
        pt.start();
        ct.start();
    }
}
```

Run the driver. You will get output that is similar to this:

```
Consumer Thread starting

Consumer Thread going to wait

Producer Thread starting

Producer Thread produced: 77

Producer Thread produced: 6

Producer Thread produced: 90
```

```
Producer Thread going to wait

Consumer Thread consumed: 77

Consumer Thread consumed: 6

Consumer Thread consumed: 90

Consumer Thread going to wait

Producer Thread produced: 56

Producer Thread produced: 89

Producer Thread produced: 3

Producer Thread ending

Consumer Thread consumed: 56

Consumer Thread consumed: 89

Consumer Thread consumed: 3

Consumer Thread ending
```

Notice the beauty of wait() notifyAll() to lock and unlock the ArrayList at appropriate time.

Types of Threads

There are two types of threads available in Java:

a). User Thread: Threads we have seen so far – threads that run in the foreground.

b). Daemon: A daemon thread is a thread that runs for the benefit of other threads. Daemon threads run in the background when processor time is available that would otherwise go to waste. The garbage collector is a daemon thread. We designate a thread as a daemon with the method call: setDaemon(true)

The setDaemon() method call must be made before the start() method of the thread is called otherwise an IllegalThreadStateException is thrown.

You can check whether a thread is daemon by calling the isDaemon() method. When all the user threads return, all the daemon threads are stopped, and the application completes execution even if the daemon threads are in the middle of processing.

Volatile

In a multi-threaded environment, if the methods are not synchronized, then multiple threads can potentially modify a field during execution. To make sure that each thread reads the most current value of these fields every time they are being used, you should mark these fields as volatile. Declaring a field volatile forces Java to reread the value of the field before use. However, volatile is not a substitute for synchronization.

Chapter 12

Networking

Unlike social networking, Computer Networking is all about transferring data from point A to point B. Raw data is put into a packet with "to" and "from" addresses on it. This is, in a nutshell, the Internet Protocol or IP. If the data is lot more than the size of a packet, we break up our data into many packets and send these successive packets. These packets are called "User Datagrams" (like telegrams in the postal service).

User Datagrams (also known as IP Datagrams) can be sent across the Internet using the User Datagram Protocol(UDP). UDP is like sending a mail using regular postal service. IP, on the other hand, is like the process that the post office follows to route and deliver the packets. Together they make UDP/IP protocol.

When you send several packets to the same address using the regular postal service, the packets might arrive in any order, some of them might be delayed, or even get lost. This is true for UDP too. You kiss goodbye to your packets and keep your fingers crossed. You have no idea whether they will reach the destination or when and how they will arrive - even if they did. Unlike the regular postal service, UDP delivers packets very fast.

Uncertain delivery is equally undesirable for postal mail as well as User Datagrams. In the case of postal mails, we deal with this problem by sending registered mail with acknowledgement. A similar protocol is used for networking to guarantee reliable delivery in the order in which packets are sent. This additional protocol is known as Transmission Control Protocol (TCP). Together, they make TCP/IP protocol. However, the transmission of packets using TCP is more like a phone call than a mail delivery - a real end-to-end connection is held open for the duration of the transmission session.

The access object at each end-point of a UDP/IP or TCP/IP connection is a Socket much like the access object at each end-point of phone conversion is a telephone set. There are, in fact, two different types of sockets: datagram socket for UDP/IP and TCP socket for TCP/IP.

IP can deliver packets in one of the following ways:

a). Fast unreliable packets via UDP (using a datagram socket). Normally, there is no connection open between the client and the server. However, it is possible to open a connection.

b). Slower, fussier but reliable packets using TCP (using TCP socket)

c). Fast raw bits using ICMP (Internet Control Message Protocol) datagrams. ICMP is more of an administrative protocol and Java does not support it.

Client-Server Model

In networking between two machines, one obviously must initiate the communication. This machine would be tagged at Client for the entire duration of the communication. The machine that is responding to the Client is tagged as Server for the entire duration of the Communication.

IP Address and Port Number

The communication between two end points is based on IP address and port number. An IP address is like a telephone number of an office and a port number is like an extension that each employee gets in the office. To give you another analogy, assume for a moment that everyone lives in apartment buildings. The street address of each apartment complex would be the IP address and the apartment number would be the port number. Every machine connected to the internet should have unique IP address. A single server may (and certainly does) provide many different services at the same time using many port numbers. Examples of these services are like Web Pages, File Transfer etc.

To request a service from the server, the client must know the IP address of the server and the port number for the service. Port numbers under 1024 are reserved for system software use.

For example, Port # 23 is the telnet service, Port #80 is HTTP service etc.

IP Address and DNS

Numbers are hard to remember, particularly a long number like IP address. In the real world, when a client requests a service (such a retrieving a Web page from the HTTP service of a server), it uses symbolic address such as www.nyu.edu rather than an IP address. There will be a Domain Name Server (DNS) locally available to the client that resolves the symbolic name into an IP address and returns it to client.

InetAddress Class

Java provides a class called InetAddress in java.net package that represents an IP address. Surprisingly, the class does not have a public constructor. Instead, it has a static method getByName() that returns an instance of InetAddress object. The method getByName() takes symbolic name (like www.nyu.edu) as argument and returns an InetAddress object that represents the IP address of the symbolic name. If you provide a symbolic name that the DNS server cannot resolve to an IP address, it throws an UnKnownHostException.

Once you receive an InetAddress object back you can call its toString() method that returns the IP address and server name. In addition, it has getHostName() that return the host name and getHostAddress() method that returns the IP Address in "x.x.x.x" format.

InetAddress has a static getLocalHost() method that returns another InetAddress object that represents the IP address of the machine that you are using. Here are some useful methods of InetAddress:

getByName(String host)	static InetAddress	Determines the IP address of a host, given the host's name.
getAllByName(String host)	static InetAddress[]	Determines all the IP addresses of a host, given the host's name.

getLocalHost()	static InetAddress	Returns the local host.
toString()	String	Converts this IP address to a String.
getHostAddress()	String	Returns the IP address string "%d.%d.%d.%d".
getHostName()	String	Returns the hostname for this address.
getAddress()	byte[]	Returns the raw IP address of this InetAddress object.

Here is an example of using it:

```java
import java.net.InetAddress;
import java.net.UnknownHostException;

public class DisplayIP{
    public static void main(String[] args){
        try
        {
            InetAddress localIP = InetAddress.getLocalHost();
            // print information about the user's local machine.
            System.out.println("Local Machine Name: " +
localIP.getHostName());
            System.out.println("Local IP Address: " +
localIP.getHostAddress());

            // use the first command line argument to create an InetAddress
object.

            InetAddress remoteIP = InetAddress.getByName("www.google.com");

            // print information about remote host name or ip address.
            System.out.println("Remote Server Name: " +
```

```
remoteIP.getHostName());
                System.out.println("Remote IP Address: " +
remoteIP.getHostAddress());


            }
            catch (UnknownHostException e){
                e.printStackTrace();
            }
        }
}
```

Here is the output from my machine:

```
Local Machine Name: CSC-HXXDV-L
Local IP Address: 192.168.2.3
Remote Server Name: www.google.com
Remote IP Address: 172.217.10.100
```

UDP/IP Client/Server

In the UDP/IP Client/Server model, both client and server send and receive unreliable datagram packets using Datagram Sockets. This is a "fire and forget" model where no acknowledgement is expected.

Using a Datagram Socket, the UDP server listens to a UDP port number (that is already advertised to its potential clients). The server is simply waiting for packets to arrive from any client.

The UDP client uses a Datagram Socket that is bound to a local UDP port number by the system. The client puts three things: a) the data, b) server IP address and c) server port number in a Datagram Packet. The Datagram Socket then sends the Datagram Packet and forgets about it.

The UDP server, on the other hand, holds an empty Datagram Packet hoping to store client data. Once the data arrives, the empty Datagram Packet at the server end is magically filled with client data and the server can get to the data as well as the client's IP address and port number by examining the Datagram Packet.

The Server can then – if it wishes to - send a response back to the client using another Datagram Packet – the same way the client did. The Client can do the same again too. This data exchange between client and server can go on for as long as they wish.

DatagramPacket Class

This class implements a "packet" of data that may be sent or received over the network through a DatagramSocket. There are two useful constructors of DatagramPacket:

Useful Constructors	
`DatagramPacket(byte[] data, int length, InetAddress address, int port)`	Client initially uses this constructor. It constructs a datagram packet for sending data using an array of bytes, size of the array, Server's IP Address and port number. The Server later can use this constructor if it decides to send response back to the Client.
`DatagramPacket(byte[] data, int length)`	Server initially uses this constructor. It constructs a DatagramPacket for receiving data using an empty array of bytes and size of the array. The Client later can use this constructor if it expects to receive response from the Server.

Here are use methods of DatagramPacket:

Useful Methods		
getAddress()	InetAddress	Returns the IP address of the machine to which this datagram is being sent or from which the datagram was received. In other words, it returns the IP Address of the other machine, not this machine.
getPort()	int	Returns the port number on the remote host to which this datagram is being sent or from which the datagram was received. In other words, it returns the port number of the other machine not this machine.
getData()	byte[]	Returns the data received or the data to be sent.
getLength()	int	Returns the length of the data to be sent or the length of the data received.

DatagramSocket Class

This class represents a socket for sending and receiving datagram packets. A datagram socket is the sending or receiving point for a packet delivery service. Each packet sent or received on a datagram socket is individually addressed and routed. Multiple packets sent from one machine to another may be routed differently and may arrive in any order. Both client and server use DatagramSocket for UDP data transmission.

Useful Constructors	
DatagramSocket()	Client uses this constructor. Constructs a datagram socket and binds it to any available port on the local host machine. Client uses it since it does not care what local port number is assigned to it.
DatagramSocket(int port)	Server uses this constructor. Constructs a datagram socket and binds it to the specified port on the local host machine. Server uses it since it already promised the client that it will be active in service with a specific port number.

Here are some useful methods of DatagramPacket:

Useful Methods		
send(DatagramPacket p)	void	Sends data in the DatagramPacket
receive(DatagramPacket p)	void	Receives incoming data into the DatagramPacket.
getInetAddress()	InetAddress	Returns the remote IP address to which this socket is connected.
getLocalAddress()	InetAddress	Gets the local IP address to which the socket is bound.
getPort()	int	Returns the remote port to which this socket is connected. Returns -1 if the socket is not connected.
getLocalPort()	int	Returns the local port number on the local host to which this socket is bound.
close()	void	Closes this datagram socket.

UDP/IP socketed connection is best demonstrated using two or more machines and I highly encourage you to do so. For now, we will use the same machine as the client and server for simplicity. Here is the server code:

```java
import java.io.IOException;
import java.net.DatagramPacket;
import java.net.DatagramSocket;


public class UDPServer{
        public static void main(String[] args){


                byte[] clientRawData = null;
                String clientStringData =null;
                DatagramPacket clientPacket=null;
                int serverPort = 12345;
                DatagramSocket serverSocket=null;

                try{


                        serverSocket = new DatagramSocket(serverPort);

                        // infinite loop
                        while (true)

                        {
                                // initialize byte array for Client.
                                clientRawData = new byte[256];


                                /* create an empty packet using empty byte array
                                for receiving client data.
                                */
                                clientPacket= new
DatagramPacket(clientRawData,clientRawData.length);


                                // print wait state.
                                System.out.println("Waiting for any client ...");
```

```
                                /* wait in receive mode.
                                     your code will block here until the
                                     server receive a packet from a client.
                                */
                                serverSocket.receive(clientPacket);

                                // print as soon as receive occurs.
                                System.out.println("Received a Packet from Client IP
Address: " + clientPacket.getAddress().getHostAddress());
                                System.out.println("Received a Packet from Client Port:
" + clientPacket.getPort());


                                // Let's get the client data and convert to string.
                                clientStringData=new String(clientPacket.getData());


                                // get rid of leading and trailing spaces.
                                clientStringData = clientStringData.trim();
                                System.out.println("Received Client Data: " +
clientStringData);
                        }
                }
                // catch exceptions.
                catch (IOException e){
                        e.printStackTrace();
                    }

                //close the socket
                finally{
                        if (!(serverSocket==null)){
                            serverSocket.close();
                        }
                    }
            }
        }
}
```

Notice the server has bound itself to port: 12345. Our client must use this port to talk to the server. You can go ahead and run the server in Eclipse, the code will get stuck on the receive() method of the socket and display the following:

```
Waiting for any client ...
```

Now, time to code the client. Here it is:

```java
import java.io.IOException;
import java.net.DatagramPacket;
import java.net.DatagramSocket;
import java.net.InetAddress;
import java.net.UnknownHostException;
public class UDPClient{
    public static void main(String[] args){

        // byte array for Client Data that will be send
        byte[] clientRawData = null;

        // String to convert byte array to string - client data.
        String clientStringData = null;

        //socket.
        DatagramSocket clientSocket = null;

        // packet for client send data.
        DatagramPacket clientPacket = null;

        try{

            // server's IP and port
            InetAddress serverIP = InetAddress.getByName("localhost");
            int serverPort = 12345;

            /* create a socket object for the client.
            notice the datagramSocket is not using the IPAddress
            or the port number - those will be used in the outgoing packet.
            */
            clientSocket = new DatagramSocket();

            // show the client port number assigned by the system
            System.out.println("Local Port: " + clientSocket.getLocalPort());
```

```
                    /* create a packet using user input,
                    server IP address and server port number.
                    the packet is signed, sealed and ready
                    to be delivered - if you know what I mean.
                    */
                    int random = (int)(Math.random()*100);
                    clientStringData = "Hello Server, sending random number: " +
random;

                    clientRawData=clientStringData.getBytes();

                    clientPacket= new DatagramPacket(clientRawData,
                    clientRawData.length,serverIP,serverPort);
                    System.out.println("Sending to Server: " + "\"" +
clientStringData
                                    + "\"" + " at IP Address: "
                                    + clientPacket.getAddress().getHostAddress()
                                    + " at Port: " + clientPacket.getPort());

                            // send the packet using the socket
                            clientSocket.send(clientPacket);
                            // the packet is out there - looking for the server
                    }
                    // catch exceptions.
                    catch (UnknownHostException e){
                            e.printStackTrace();
                    }
                    catch (IOException e){
                            e.printStackTrace();
                    }
                    // close the socket
                    finally{
                        if (!(clientSocket==null)){
                                clientSocket.close();
                        }
                    }
                }
            }
        }
```

Notice the client is going to send the packet to "localhost" which means "this machine" at port: 12345. That's exactly the port that our server is listening to. It is best to run the client from a command prompt so that we can see activities on both sides on separate console. Here are the steps:

1). In Eclipse, right click on the project and select properties. In properties window find the location. Copy the location. In my case the location is: C:\Users\rahmanm\workspace\ CCJChapter12

2). Press Windows button and type +r to find the run command. Type: cmd and press enter key

3). A black command prompt will pop up

4). Type CD, press spacebar, type ", then press control+v(paste), type ". In my case it is: cd "C:\Users\rahmanm\workspace\CCJChapter12"

5). You will see that your current director has changed to the project location

6). Type: CD bin

7). You will see that you are in bin folder of the project

8). Type: dir

9). You should see UDPClient.class as one of the files in the folder

10). Now type: Java UDPClient

Client code will run and you will see output like this:

```
Local Port: 62620

Sending to Server: "Hello Server, sending random number: 49" at IP Address:
127.0.0.1 at Port: 12345
```

Here is a picture of my command prompt:

```
C:\Users\rahmanm>cd
C:\Users\rahmanm

C:\Users\rahmanm>cd "C:\Users\rahmanm\workspace\CCJChapter12"

C:\Users\rahmanm\workspace\CCJChapter12>cd bin

C:\Users\rahmanm\workspace\CCJChapter12\bin>dir
 Volume in drive C is Windows OS
 Volume Serial Number is 5218-8003

 Directory of C:\Users\rahmanm\workspace\CCJChapter12\bin

11/30/2018  12:03 AM    <DIR>          .
11/30/2018  12:03 AM    <DIR>          ..
11/29/2018  04:23 PM             1,338 DisplayIP.class
11/30/2018  12:39 AM             2,364 UDPClient.class
11/30/2018  02:35 PM             1,959 UDPServer.class
               3 File(s)          5,661 bytes
               2 Dir(s)  290,969,128,960 bytes free

C:\Users\rahmanm\workspace\CCJChapter12\bin>Java UDPClient
Local Port: 62620
Sending to Server: "Hello Server, sending random number: 49" at IP Address: 127.0.0.1 at Port: 12345

C:\Users\rahmanm\workspace\CCJChapter12\bin>
```

This basically shows that the client sent the data to the server. The real beauty is on the server side. Go back to server console in Eclipse and check it. Here is the output now:

```
Received a Packet from Client IP Address: 127.0.0.1
Received a Packet from Client Port: 62620
Received Client Data: Hello Server, sending random number: 49
Waiting for any client ...
```

Congratulations!!!

You have successfully communicated with the server. Run the client again by typing:

Java UDPClient

You will get similar output on both end, only the random number will change.

Open another command prompt by following the steps and type: Java UDPClient on the new command prompt. You will see that server will receive that data too, except the client port number will be different.

By the way, the server is running in an infinite loop. You need to kill the server at some point by pressing the red square at the bottom right side of Eclipse next to x and xx symbol and just above the console.

TCP/IP Client/Server

TCP/IP Socket connections also works with the same client-server model. Initially the Server keeps listening for incoming requests at a certain port number using special type of socket called ServerSocket. It uses the accept() method of ServerSocket for listening.

The client initiates a connection using Socket (not DatagramSocket, this is a TCP Socket). As soon as the client hits the server, the accept() method on the server returns a Socket(same type of TCP Socket on the client side, not ServerSocket) object. The new Socket object on the server is bound to a different port number assigned by the system (the client does not need to know about this new port number at all – the transfer from the original port to this new port is transparent to the client) and connects client to it. The server needs this new socket (and consequently a different port number) so that it can continue to listen using the original ServerSocket for other incoming clients while providing service for the connected clients.

The best way to describe this is using an analogy. Image you are calling the 800 number for Home Shopping Network. Your phone is a Socket and the 800 number is the ServerSocket. As soon as you got connected to the 800 number you are automatically transferred to a phone belonging to the next available representative. The representative's phone is like a regular Socket as yours. The 800 number (ServerSocket) is still available for the next client to call.

Reading and Writing to Sockets

In Java, for simplicity, TCP/IP sockets read/write are made to look like regular I/O streams. In other word, a TCP/IP socket works like a file that you can read from and write to. You simply read and write data using the usual stream methods and it automatically appears at the other end. A socket supports two-way communication at the same time. There is a method getInputStream() to get to the input stream of a socket and another method getOutputStream() to get to the output stream. This allows the client and the server to talk back and forth.

The ServerSocket Class

A ServerSocket waits for requests to come in over the network from a client. When you create a ServerSocket, it listens for connection requests on a specified port. When a connection request arrives, the accept() method of the ServerSocket accepts the requested client and returns a Socket object for future communication between the client and the server. The ServerSocket then goes back to listening mode for other incoming client requests.

The Socket Class

This class implements client sockets. A Socket is an endpoint for communication between two machines. It has a constructor that takes a) the IP address of the server and b) the port number of the server and connects to it. The constructors can throw UnknownHostException and IOException if there is any problem with the connection.

Useful Methods		
getInputStream()	InputStream	Returns an input stream for this socket.
getOutputStream()	OutputStream	Returns an output stream for this socket.
getInetAddress()	InetAddress	Returns the address to which the socket is connected.
getLocalAddress()	InetAddress	Gets the local address to which the socket is bound.

getPort()	int	Returns the remote port to which this socket is connected.
getLocalPort()	int	Returns the local port to which this socket is bound.
close()	void	Closes this socket.

Here is a TCPServer:

```java
import java.io.BufferedReader;
import java.io.IOException;
import java.io.InputStream;
import java.io.InputStreamReader;
import java.net.ServerSocket;
import java.net.Socket;


public class TCPServer{
     public static void main(String[] args){
          // String to store - client data.
          String clientData = null;

          // to store server port number received as command line argument.
          int serverPort = 54321;


          // socket variables
          ServerSocket serverSocket = null;
          Socket socket = null;

          // variables for wrapping input stream
          InputStream inputStream = null;
          InputStreamReader inputStreamReader = null;
          BufferedReader bufferedReader = null;

          try{
```

```
/* create a server socket object with
server port number
*/
serverSocket = new ServerSocket(serverPort);


//print server port
System.out.println("Server Port #: " +
serverSocket.getLocalPort());


// print before wait.
System.out.println("Waiting for Client connection ...");

while(true){ //infinite loop
    /* wait for the client
    your code will block here
    until a client connects.
    */
    socket = serverSocket.accept();

    // print after connection.
    System.out.println("Client connected.");

    // show client IP info.
    System.out.println("Client IP Address #: " +
socket.getInetAddress().getHostAddress());

    // show client port info.
    System.out.println("Client Port #: " + socket.getPort());

    // get the input stream of the socket.
    inputStream = socket.getInputStream();

    // convert byte stream to character stream.
    inputStreamReader = new InputStreamReader(inputStream);

    // buffer character stream.
    bufferedReader = new BufferedReader(inputStreamReader);

    clientData = bufferedReader.readLine();
```

```
                    // print client input.
                    System.out.println("Client Input: " + clientData);

                    //close the socket now
                    socket.close();
                }
            }
            // catch exceptions.
            catch (IOException e){
                e.printStackTrace();
            }
    // close the outermost wrappers and socket
    finally{
            try{
                if (!(bufferedReader==null)){bufferedReader.close();}
                if (!(socket==null) && !(socket.isClosed())){socket.close();}
                if (!(serverSocket==null)){serverSocket.close();}
            }
            catch(Exception e){
                e.printStackTrace();
            }
        }
    }
}
```

Run the server on Eclipse

Here is the TCP Client:

```
import java.io.IOException;
import java.io.OutputStream;
import java.io.OutputStreamWriter;
import java.io.PrintWriter;
import java.net.InetAddress;
import java.net.Socket;
import java.net.UnknownHostException;

public class TCPClient{
```

```
public static void main(String[] args){
        String clientData = null;

        // to store server port number received as command line argument.
        int serverPort = 54321;

        // to store server IP address
        InetAddress serverIP = null;

        // for client socket
        Socket clientSocket = null;

        //variables to wrapup the outputstream of the socket
        OutputStream socketOutputStream = null;
        OutputStreamWriter socketOutputStreamWriter = null;
        PrintWriter socketPrintWriter = null;

        try{
            serverIP = InetAddress.getByName("localhost");

            // create a socket object with server IP Address
            // and server port number
            clientSocket = new Socket(serverIP,serverPort);

            // show the client port number assigned automatically

            System.out.println("Client IP Address: " +
clientSocket.getLocalAddress().getHostAddress());
            System.out.println("Client Port #: " +
clientSocket.getLocalPort());

            // show server info.
            System.out.println("Server IP Address: " +
clientSocket.getInetAddress().getHostAddress());
            System.out.println("Server Port #: " + clientSocket.getPort());

            int random = (int)(Math.random()*100);
            clientData = "Hello Server, sending random number: " + random;

            // print before send
            System.out.println("Sending data to the server: " + clientData);
```

```
                // get the output stream of the socket.
                socketOutputStream = clientSocket.getOutputStream();

                // convert byte stream to character stream.
                socketOutputStreamWriter = new
OutputStreamWriter(socketOutputStream);

                // Convert to PrintWriter so that we can use println() method.
                socketPrintWriter = new PrintWriter(socketOutputStreamWriter);

                // send the data to the server
                socketPrintWriter.println(clientData);

                //flush the output since it is buffered.
                socketPrintWriter.flush();
                socketPrintWriter.close();
        }
        // catch exceptions.
        catch (UnknownHostException e){
                e.printStackTrace();
        }
        catch (IOException e){
                e.printStackTrace();
        }
    // close the outermost wrappers and socket
    finally{
            try{
                if (!(socketPrintWriter==null)){socketPrintWriter.close();}
                if (!(clientSocket==null)){clientSocket.close();}
            }
            catch(Exception e){
                System.out.println(e);
            }
    }

    }
}
```

Run the client from the same command prompt as you did for udp client by typing:

Java TCPClent

You will get output like UPD client. On Eclipse's command prompt you will see that the server did receive the message.

Open another command prompt and run another client. You will see similar output.

In Eclipse the server will keep running until you kill it by clicking on the red square as you did before for UDP server.

Now let's focus on two-way communication. Here is the scenario. The client will prompt you to enter your name. It will then send your name to the server. The server will reply with "Hello" followed by your name in all uppercase. The client then will prompt you for your name again. You will enter another name. The server will say hello again. This will keep on going until you hit just enter instead of typing your name.

Here is the Server:

```java
import java.io.BufferedReader;
import java.io.IOException;
import java.io.InputStream;
import java.io.InputStreamReader;
import java.io.OutputStream;
import java.io.OutputStreamWriter;
import java.io.PrintWriter;
import java.net.ServerSocket;
import java.net.Socket;


public class TCPHelloServer{
    public static void main(String[] args){
```

```java
        // String to store - client data.
        String clientData = null;

        // String to store - server data.
        String serverData = null;

        //loop variable
        boolean forever=true;

        // to store server port number received as command line argument.
        int serverPort = 56789;



        // socket variables
        ServerSocket serverSocket = null;
        Socket socket = null;

        // variables for wrapping input stream
        InputStream inputStream = null;
        InputStreamReader inputStreamReader = null;
        BufferedReader bufferedReader = null;

        // variables for wrapping output stream
        OutputStream outputStream = null;
        OutputStreamWriter outputStreamWriter = null;
        PrintWriter printWriter = null;



        try{

            /* create a server socket object with
            server port number
            */
            serverSocket = new ServerSocket(serverPort);

            //print server port
            System.out.println("Server Port #: " +
serverSocket.getLocalPort());
```

```java
            while(true){ //infinite loop

                    // print before wait.
                    System.out.println("Waiting for Client connection ...");

                    /* wait for the client
                    your code will block here
                    until a client connects.
                    */

                    socket = serverSocket.accept();

                    // print after connection.
                    System.out.println("Client connected.");

                    // show client IP info.
                    System.out.println("Client IP Address #: " +
socket.getInetAddress().getHostAddress());

                    // show client port info.
                    System.out.println("Client Port #: " + socket.getPort());

                    // get the input stream of the socket.
                    inputStream = socket.getInputStream();

                    // convert byte stream to character stream.
                    inputStreamReader = new InputStreamReader(inputStream);

                    // buffer character stream.
                    bufferedReader = new BufferedReader(inputStreamReader);

                    // get the output stream of the socket.
                    outputStream = socket.getOutputStream();

                    // convert byte stream to character stream.
                    outputStreamWriter = new
OutputStreamWriter(outputStream);
```

```
                          // Convert to PrintWriter so that we can use println()
method.

                          printWriter = new PrintWriter(outputStreamWriter);


                          while (forever){
                              clientData = bufferedReader.readLine();


                              //if empty user input - exit loop.
                              if ((clientData==null) || (clientData.trim().
length()==0)){

                                  bufferedReader.close();
                                  printWriter.close();
                                  socket.close();
                                  forever=false;
                                  break;
                              }



                              // print client input.
                              System.out.println("Client Input: " + clientData);

                              //convert to upper case
                              serverData = "Hello " + clientData.toUpperCase();

                              // print before send
                              System.out.println("Sending data to the client: " +
serverData);


                              // send the data to the client
                              printWriter.println(serverData);

                              //flush the output since it is buffered.

                              printWriter.flush();


                          }
                      }
                  }
                  // catch exceptions.
                  catch (IOException e){
```

```
                        e.printStackTrace();
                }
                // close the outermost wrappers and socket
                finally{
                    try{
                        if (!(bufferedReader==null)){bufferedReader.close();}
                        if (!(printWriter==null)){printWriter.close();}
                        if (!(socket==null) && !(socket.isClosed())){socket.close();}
                        if (!(serverSocket==null)){serverSocket.close();}
                    }
                    catch(Exception e){
                        e.printStackTrace();
                    }
                }
        }
    }
}
```

Run the server on Eclipse.

Here is your client:

```
import java.io.BufferedReader;

import java.io.BufferedWriter;

import java.io.IOException;

import java.io.InputStream;

import java.io.InputStreamReader;

import java.io.OutputStream;

import java.io.OutputStreamWriter;

import java.io.PrintWriter;

import java.net.InetAddress;

import java.net.Socket;

import java.net.UnknownHostException;

public class TCPHelloClient{
```

```
public static void main(String[] args){
    // String to store - client data.
    String clientData = null;

    // String to store - server data.
    String serverData = null;

    // to store server port number received as command line argument.
    int serverPort = 56789;

    // to store server IP address
    InetAddress serverIP = null;

    // for client socket
    Socket clientSocket = null;

    // variables to wrapup System.in
    InputStreamReader systemInputStreamReader = null;
    BufferedReader systemBufferedReader = null;

    //variables to wrapup inputstream of the socket
    InputStream socketInputStream = null;
    InputStreamReader socketInputReader = null;
    BufferedReader socketBufferedReader = null;


    //variables to wrapup the outputstream of the socket
    OutputStream socketOutputStream = null;
    OutputStreamWriter socketOutputStreamWriter = null;
    PrintWriter socketPrintWriter = null;

    try{
            serverIP = InetAddress.getByName("localhost");


            /* create a socket object with server IP Address
            and server port number
            */
            clientSocket = new Socket(serverIP,serverPort);

            // show the client port number assigned automatically
            System.out.println("Client IP Address: " + clientSocket.
```

```
getLocalAddress().getHostAddress());
            System.out.println("Client Port #: " + clientSocket.getLocalPort());

            // show server info.
            System.out.println("Server IP Address: " + clientSocket.
getInetAddress().getHostAddress());
            System.out.println("Server Port #: " + clientSocket.getPort());

            // get the input stream of the socket.
            socketInputStream = clientSocket.getInputStream();

            // convert byte stream to character stream.
            socketInputReader = new InputStreamReader(socketInputStream);

            // buffer character stream.
            socketBufferedReader = new BufferedReader(socketInputReader);

            // get the output stream of the socket.
            socketOutputStream = clientSocket.getOutputStream();

            // convert byte stream to character stream.
            socketOutputStreamWriter = new
OutputStreamWriter(socketOutputStream);

            // Convert to PrintWriter so that we can use println() method.
            socketPrintWriter = new PrintWriter(socketOutputStreamWriter);

            // convert byte stream to character stream - keyboard input.
            systemInputStreamReader = new InputStreamReader(System.in);

            // buffer character stream - keyboard input.
            systemBufferedReader = new
BufferedReader(systemInputStreamReader);
            // infinite loop
            while (true)
            {
                    // prompt user to input
                    System.out.print("Enter your name: ");

                    // get user input
                    clientData=systemBufferedReader.readLine();
```

```
                    //exit if the user hits just <Enter>
                    if (clientData.length()==0)
                    {
                            return;
                    }

                    // print before send
                    System.out.println("Sending data to the server: " +
clientData);

                    // send the data to the server
                    socketPrintWriter.println(clientData);

                    //flush the output since it is buffered.
                    socketPrintWriter.flush();

                    // print before receive
                    System.out.println("Waiting for the server ...");

                    /* waiting for the server response.
                    code will block here until we hear back from the server
                    */
                    serverData = socketBufferedReader.readLine();

                    // print server response
                    System.out.println("Server Response: " + serverData);

                }
            }
            // catch exceptions.
            catch (UnknownHostException e){
                    e.printStackTrace();
            }
            catch (IOException e){
                    e.printStackTrace();
            }
        // close the outermost wrappers and socket
        finally{
            try{
                    if (!(systemBufferedReader==null)){systemBufferedReader.close();}
                    if (!(socketBufferedReader==null)){socketBufferedReader.close();}
                    if (!(socketPrintWriter==null)){socketPrintWriter.close();}
```

```
                    if (!(clientSocket==null)){clientSocket.close();}
        }
        catch(Exception e){
                System.out.println(e);
        }
    }


    }
}
```

Run your client on command prompt. Enter your name. You will get "Hello" response as follows:

```
Server Port #: 56789
Waiting for Client connection ...
Client connected.
Client IP Address #: 127.0.0.1
Client Port #: 52241
Thread Thread-0 started
Waiting for the client input ...
Client Input: John
Sending data to the client: Hello JOHN
Waiting for the client input ...
```

You can keep entering one name after another and you will get response every time. A problem arises after you run a second client on a second command prompt. Everything will seem to go well up until you enter your name. Then you will get no response. Your code will hang as follows:

```
Client IP Address: 127.0.0.1
Client Port #: 52396
Server IP Address: 127.0.0.1
Server Port #: 56789
Enter your name: Jay
Sending data to the server: Jay
Waiting for the server ...
```

You will never hear back from the server from the second client. Why? Well, the problem is not on the client side but rather on the server side. Our server is engaging into a conversion with the first client which disables it to talk to another client.

So, how do we solve this problem? We have to bring threads in the mix. The idea is, as soon as a client arrives, the server will create a brand new thread and hand off the socket to the thread. The new thread will do all the I/O with the client keeping the server free for the next client.

Here is our new multi-threaded server:

```java
import java.io.IOException;
import java.net.ServerSocket;
import java.net.Socket;

public class TCPThreadedHelloServer{
    public static void main(String[] args){

        // to store server port number received as command line argument.
        int serverPort = 44444;

        // socket variables
        ServerSocket serverSocket = null;
        Socket socket = null;

        try{

            // create a server socket object with
            // server port number
            serverSocket = new ServerSocket(serverPort);

            //print server port
            System.out.println("Server Port #: " +
serverSocket.getLocalPort());
```

```
                // print before wait.
                System.out.println("Waiting for Client connection ...");

                /* wait for the client
                your code will block here
                until a client connects.
                */
                while(true){
                    socket = serverSocket.accept();

                    // print after connection.
                    System.out.println("Client connected.");

                    // show client IP info.
                    System.out.println("Client IP Address #: " +
socket.getInetAddress().getHostAddress());

                    // show client port info.
                    System.out.println("Client Port #: " + socket.getPort());
                    TCPHelloServerThread thread = new
TCPHelloServerThread(socket);
                    thread.start();
                    System.out.println("Thread " + thread.getName() + "
started");
                }
            }
            // catch exceptions.
            catch (IOException e){
                e.printStackTrace();
            }
            // close the outermost wrappers and socket
            finally{
            try{
                if (!(socket==null)){socket.close();}
                if (!(serverSocket==null)){serverSocket.close();}
            }
            catch(Exception e){
                e.printStackTrace();
            }
        }
    }
}
```

Notice the server is using 44444 port and it is handing off the socket to a thread.

And here is the thread:

```java
import java.io.BufferedReader;

import java.io.IOException;

import java.io.InputStream;

import java.io.InputStreamReader;

import java.io.OutputStream;

import java.io.OutputStreamWriter;

import java.io.PrintWriter;

import java.net.Socket;


public class TCPHelloServerThread extends Thread {
    private Socket socket;

    public TCPHelloServerThread(Socket anySocket){
        socket = anySocket;
    }
    public void run(){

        // String to store - server data.
        String serverData = null;

        // String to store - client data.
        String clientData = null;


        //loop variable
        boolean forever=true;


        // variables for wrapping input stream
        InputStream inputStream = null;
```

```java
InputStreamReader inputStreamReader = null;
BufferedReader bufferedReader = null;

// variables for wrapping output stream
OutputStream outputStream = null;
OutputStreamWriter outputStreamWriter = null;
PrintWriter printWriter = null;


try{
        // get the input stream of the socket.
        inputStream = socket.getInputStream();

        // convert byte stream to character stream.
        inputStreamReader = new InputStreamReader(inputStream);

        // buffer character stream.
        bufferedReader = new BufferedReader(inputStreamReader);

        // get the output stream of the socket.
        outputStream = socket.getOutputStream();

        // convert byte stream to character stream.
        outputStreamWriter = new OutputStreamWriter(outputStream);

        // Convert to PrintWriter so that we can use println() method.
        printWriter = new PrintWriter(outputStreamWriter);

        while (forever){
                // print before receive
                System.out.println("Waiting for the client input ...");

                //waiting for the client input.
                // your code will block here ustil
                // snd home data from the client
                clientData = bufferedReader.readLine();

                //if empty user input - exit loop.
                if ((clientData==null) || (clientData.trim().length()==0)){
                        forever=false;
                        bufferedReader.close();
                        printWriter.close();
```

```
                        socket.close();
                        break;
            }

            // print client input.
            System.out.println("Client Input: " + clientData);

            //convert to upper case
            serverData = "Hello " + clientData.toUpperCase();

            // print before send
            System.out.println("Sending data to the client: " +
serverData);

            // send the data to the client
            printWriter.println(serverData);

            //flush the output since it is buffered.
            printWriter.flush();
        }
    }
    // catch exceptions.
    catch (IOException e){
            e.printStackTrace();
    }
    // close the outermost wrappers and socket
    finally{
        try{
            if (!(bufferedReader==null)){bufferedReader.close();}
            if (!(printWriter==null)){printWriter.close();}
            if (!(socket==null)){socket.close();}
        }
        catch(Exception e){
            e.printStackTrace();
        }
    }

}

}
```

Notice how the thread is engaged in all the data exchange back and forth with the client.

We don't need to change the client at all except for the port number for the server. To avoid any confusion, we will copy the TCPHelloClient to TCPHelloClientForThread and change to port number in the code as follows:

```
int serverPort = 44444;
```

Let's run the server in Eclipse.

Let's run the first client from command prompt as follows:

```
Java TCPHelloClientForThread
```

Enter John as name, we will get the following output:

```
Client IP Address: 127.0.0.1
Client Port #: 52516
Server IP Address: 127.0.0.1
Server Port #: 44444
Enter your name: John
Sending data to the server: John
Waiting for the server ...
Server Response: Hello JOHN
Enter your name:
```

Let's open another command prompt and type:

```
Java TCPHelloClientForThread
```

Enter Barbara as name, you will get the following output:

```
Client IP Address: 127.0.0.1
Client Port #: 52524
Server IP Address: 127.0.0.1
Server Port #: 44444
Enter your name: Barbara
Sending data to the server: Barbara
```

```
Waiting for the server ...
Server Response: Hello BARBARA
Enter your name:
```

Go back and forth between the two clients and keep entering different names, you will get proper response from the server.

You can stop the client by simply hitting enter. To stop the server you have to click on the red square on the bottom right side right above the console.

The End

Printed in the United States
By Bookmasters